EXPER

PRAGUE & CZECHIA

LIKE A LOCAL

A Practical Pocket Guide For All Travelers

Caleb J. Smith

Copyright © by Caleb J. Smith 2024.

All rights reserved.

Except for brief quotations used in critical reviews and other non-commercial uses permitted by copyright law, no part of this publication may be copied, distributed, or transmitted in any way without the publisher's prior written consent, including by photocopying, recording, or other electronic or mechanical methods.

The use of any trademarks or brands mentioned in this book is solely for the purpose of clarification and is not intended to imply any affiliation with the respective owners of those marks or brands.

Map of Czech Republic

Click here to View the Map of Czech Republic
(For e-book readers)

Scan the QR Code below with your mobile phone's Camera to View the Map of Czech Republic (For Paperback Readers).

TABLE OF CONTENTS

Map of Czech Republic

INTRODUCTION

Geographic Highlights

History and Culture of the Capital

CHAPTER 1

Essential Tips for Travelers

Visa Guidelines and Entry Requirements

Health and Safety Updates

What to Pack: Prague Edition

Budgeting for Your Trip: Expenses in Prague

Optimal Travel Times

Understanding Local Culture and Social Norms

Basic Czech Phrases for Travelers

CHAPTER 2

Arrival and Transportation

Arriving in Prague: Air and Rail Options

Navigating Prague: Public Transport and

Other Means

CHAPTER 3

Where to Stay

Accommodation Ranges: Luxury to Economical

Characteristic Boutique Inns and Historical Lodgings

Family-Friendly Hotels and Vacation Stays

Distinctive Stays: Heritage Properties and Agritourism Sites

Reservation Insights and Preferred Booking Platforms

CHAPTER 4

Food and Dining

Traditional Czech Dishes to Try

Premier Dining Spots in Prague

Best Restaurants for Local Flavors

Cafes and Bistros in Prague

Vegetarian and Vegan Options

Culinary Courses and Food Tours

CHAPTER 5

Shopping Insights

Marketplaces and Street Vendors

Exclusive Shops in Prague's City Center

Keepsakes: Traditional Czech Products, Regional Souvenirs and Handicrafts

CHAPTER 6

Attractions and Activities

Prague's Cultural Heritage

Notable Sites: Prague Castle, Charles Bridge, Old Town Square and the Astronomical Clock

Museums: National Museum, Mucha Museum, Museum of Communism

River Rafting and Outdoor Adventures

Adventures in the Krkonoše Mountains

Brno: The Vibrant City Life

Olomouc: The Artistic Haven

Day Trips to Karlštejn Castle and Kutná Hora

CHAPTER 7

Lesser-Known Treasures

Historical Walks: Exploring Lesser Town and Vyšehrad

Off-the-Beaten Path Cultural Sites: Bethlehem Chapel and Strahov Monastery

Discover Prague's Secluded Courtyards, and Natural Enclaves

CHAPTER 8

Southern Bohemia

Historical Sites: Český Krumlov Castle and Hluboká Castle

Discovering the Lipno Reservoir

Scenic Routes: Hiking in Šumava National Park

CHAPTER 9

Northern Bohemia

Coastal Delights: Liberec and the Jizera Mountains

Terezín Memorial and Bohemian Paradise

Nature Observations: Saxon Switzerland National Park

CHAPTER 10

Central Bohemia

Discovery and Learning: Aviation Museum Kbely

The Enigmatic Bone Church of Sedlec

Local Celebrations and Traditional Crafts in Pilsen

CHAPTER 11

Western Bohemia

Military History and Scenic Views in Cheb

Karlovy Vary: Spa Town and Film Festival

Gardens and Historic Walks: Exploring Mariánské Lázně

CHAPTER 12

Nightlife and Entertainment

Prague's Vibrant Night Scene: Clubs and Bars

Cultural Nights: Opera and Ballet at the National Theatre

Leisure and Gaming: Casinos and Interactive Experiences

Yearly Festivals: An Overview

CHAPTER 13

Activities for Different Travelers

Solo Travelers: Custom Tours and Activities

Couples: Romantic Retreats and Activities

Family Ventures: Attractions Suited for Children

Seniors: Accessible Tourism and Comfort Travel

Groups: Activities Tour

CHAPTER 14

Itineraries

Organizing Day Trips: From Prague to Nearby Gems

Brief Visits: Structured 3-Day Plans

Extensive Weeklong Journeys: A Detailed 7-Day Guide

2-Week Comprehensive Tour of the Czech Republic

CHAPTER 15

Essential Information

Internet, Communication, and Staying Connected

Free Tourist Attractions and Paid Tourist Attractions

Opening Hours for Major Attractions

Car Rental recommendations

Guided Tours vs. Self-Guided Explorations

Useful Apps and Websites

Departure Checklist and Customs Regulations

CONCLUSION

INTRODUCTION

The Czech Republic, with its rich tapestry of history, impressive architecture, and hearty cuisine, invites travelers to step into a world where medieval meets modern. This guide opens the door to a land known for its beautiful cities, enchanting forests, and a fascinating history that dates back over a millennium. Whether you're wandering through the cobblestone streets of Prague or exploring the lesser-known villages that dot the countryside, the Czech Republic offers an array of experiences that cater to every kind of traveler.

As you delve into this guide, you'll find practical advice on how to navigate this central European gem, from securing the right visa to finding the coziest spots for a warm meal. You'll learn about the best times to visit, from the golden hues of autumn to the vibrant festivals of summer. Each section provides detailed insights into everything from local customs to language tips that will help you say more than just "hello" to the friendly locals. We've organized the guide to ensure you can easily find information relevant to your trip. Whether you're looking for luxury accommodations or budget-friendly options, this book details a range of places to stay. Food lovers will relish our recommendations on where to sample traditional Czech dishes, and adventure seekers will find plenty of information on the country's outdoor activities.

Every chapter of this guide is designed to equip you with knowledge that will make your visit as smooth and enjoyable as possible. This introduction sets the stage for a journey that promises rich experiences, practical travel tips, and a deeper understanding of the Czech Republic's enduring charm. Read on to uncover all that this remarkable country has to offer, and prepare yourself for an unforgettable adventure.

Geographic Highlights

Traveling through the Czech Republic, I found myself captivated by the diverse landscapes that unfolded before me. Each region of this storied country offers unique geographical wonders that seem to tell their own tales of the natural world and human history intertwining beautifully.

Starting in the north, the Bohemian Switzerland National Park presents a spectacular showcase of what nature can sculpt over millennia. The towering sandstone cliffs and the lush gorges carved by rivers such as the Kamenice are reminiscent of a painting come to life. A hike through these rugged terrains not only tested my physical endurance but also rewarded me with breathtaking views that seemed almost too majestic to be real. The Pravčická Brána, the largest natural sandstone arch in Europe, was particularly awe-inspiring, with its vast size and striking form.

Moving southwards, the Moravian Karst was another geographic marvel that captured my fascination. This area is a paradise for spelunkers with over a thousand caves. The Punkva Caves, where I had the chance to ride a boat through subterranean rivers, offered a glimpse into an underground world that felt both eerie and enchanting. The Macocha Abyss, a sinkhole over 138 meters deep, provided a stunning view into the depths of the earth, showcasing layers of geological history.

In the heart of the country, the rolling hills and vineyards of Moravia offered a different flavor of natural beauty. The landscapes here are softer but no less impressive, with endless green fields that stretch towards the horizon, dotted with ancient castles and sleepy villages whose histories are steeped in centuries of winemaking tradition.

Each step through the Czech Republic brought me closer to understanding the deep connection the locals have with their land. From the grandiose mountains in the north to the serene valleys in the south, the geographic diversity here offers endless opportunities for exploration and appreciation. The natural beauty of this country is not just in its landscapes but also in the way these landscapes shape the culture and lifestyle of its people.

My journey through the Czech Republic taught me more than I could have imagined about the power of nature and the resilience of human history. It's a place where every landscape tells a story, and every view holds a promise of a new adventure.

History and Culture of the Capital

Walking through Prague, the capital of the Czech Republic, is like stepping into a different era. Every cobblestone, alleyway, and building tells a story, reflecting centuries of history, conflict, and celebration. As I explored this city, known as the "City of a Hundred Spires," I felt a palpable sense of the past merging seamlessly with the present.

The history of Prague is as fascinating as it is complex. Founded during the Romanesque and flourishing by the Gothic and Renaissance eras, Prague has been a political, cultural, and economic center of central Europe. The city's architecture is a testament to its storied past, with its well-preserved medieval layout complete with gothic cathedrals and baroque buildings, most notably the Prague Castle, Charles Bridge, and the Astronomical Clock, which stand as icons of the city's rich heritage. Prague Castle, perched majestically above the Vltava River, has been the seat of power for kings of Bohemia, Holy Roman emperors, and presidents of Czechoslovakia. The changing of the guard at the castle gates is a ceremony that encapsulates the pride and tradition of the Czech people. Meanwhile, crossing the Charles Bridge, with its array of statues and bustling vendors, offers a window into the daily lives of the locals and the throngs of tourists drawn by the city's charm and beauty. But Prague is not just about historical artifacts. The city throbs with a cultural beat that resonates in its numerous theaters, opera houses, and concert halls. My evenings were often spent enjoying classical music concerts or jazz sessions in some of the city's contemporary spaces, showing how the city marries its illustrious past with a dynamic and creative present.

The cultural life of Prague also extends into literature, with the city having been home to famous writers like Franz Kafka and Milan Kundera, whose works were deeply influenced by Prague's mystique and its political turmoil.

Walking through the narrow streets of the Old Town, I could almost picture Kafka wandering through these same streets, drawing inspiration for his surreal tales.

Czech cuisine also plays a significant role in Prague's cultural experience. Dining on traditional dishes like goulash, svíčková, or the famous Czech beer, I found that the food here tells its own story of regional influences and historical necessities. Each meal is a celebration of Czech heritage, served with a warmth that invites conversation and camaraderie.

As I reflect on my time in Prague, I realize that the city's true essence lies in its ability to keep its history alive, not just in monuments and museums, but in its streets, its food, and its people. Prague doesn't just belong to the Czech Republic; it belongs to the narrative of Europe, continually evolving, yet always remembering the chapters that came before.

CHAPTER 1

Essential Tips for Travelers

As you prepare to explore the Czech Republic, with its enchanting castles, storied streets, and lively culture, a few expert tips can make your journey as smooth as it is memorable. Whether it's your first visit or a return trip, knowing the essentials before you go sets the stage for a fantastic experience. This chapter will guide you through key travel advice, from visa guidelines and entry requirements to local customs that will enrich your stay.

Navigating the administrative aspects of travel can be tricky, but don't worry—I'll walk you through the latest on visa processes and what to expect when you arrive, so there are no surprises at the border. Health and safety are paramount, especially in unfamiliar places. I'll share up-to-date information to keep you safe and sound, covering everything from travel insurance recommendations to local medical facilities.

Packing for Prague or any new destination is an art. With insights into Prague's weather patterns and local fashion norms, you'll pack like a pro, ready for both the opera and the cobblestones. Managing your travel budget is also crucial. I'll offer practical advice on how to enjoy the city's delights without breaking the bank, from dining out to discovering free hidden gems. Timing your visit can greatly affect your experience. We'll discuss the best times to visit Prague to enjoy its beauty without the crowds. And to truly blend in, understanding local culture and social norms is key. From dining etiquette to navigating public transport, I'll provide the nuances that can make you feel almost like a Local. Lastly, a little language goes a long way. I'll equip you with basic Czech phrases that not only help with navigation but also open doors to friendly conversations with locals.

Visa Guidelines and Entry Requirements

When I started planning my trip to the Czech Republic, I knew that one of the most important steps was to get all the visa and entry details sorted out before packing my bags. The Czech Republic is part of the Schengen Area, which means it follows the same rules as many other European countries for travelers. This can make things simpler, but it's still essential to know the specifics to avoid any surprises at the airport.

If you're coming from a country that is part of the European Union or the Schengen Zone, you're in luck—no visa is required for your visit. Citizens of countries like Germany, France, or Italy can travel to the Czech Republic as freely as moving between cities in their own nations. However, if you're from outside the EU, things get a little more structured. For travelers from countries like the United States, Canada, or Australia, you won't need a visa for stays up to 90 days. This is great for short holidays or business trips, but you must ensure that your passport is valid for at least three months beyond your planned departure date.

For those who do need a visa, such as travelers from many African or Asian countries, the Schengen visa application process is required. I went through this process once for a previous trip to Europe, and it involves several steps, so it's wise to start early. You'll need to fill out an application form, provide recent passport-sized photos, and include proof of travel insurance that meets the Schengen minimum requirements (usually covering €30,000 in medical expenses). Additionally, you'll need documents showing your travel itinerary, accommodation bookings, and proof that you have enough funds to cover your stay. Bank statements, flight tickets, and hotel reservations typically do the trick. Arriving in the Czech Republic is usually straightforward. If you're flying into Václav Havel Airport in Prague, you can expect to go through immigration quickly, especially if you have your documents ready and meet the requirements. Border officers might ask about the purpose of your trip or how long you plan to stay, but as long as you're prepared, this part of the journey is smooth.

One detail that caught my attention is that the Czech Republic requires you to register with local authorities if you're staying for more than 30 days, but this is mostly relevant for long-term stays or study programs. For short-term tourists, this doesn't apply, but it's always good to be aware of local rules. Another important point is travel insurance. While it's a requirement for those applying for a visa, even if you don't need a visa, having travel insurance is highly recommended. I've learned from experience that it's always better to have coverage in case of unexpected issues, whether it's a medical emergency or a canceled flight. Many insurance providers offer affordable short-term policies specifically designed for trips to Europe. For travelers under 18, there are additional considerations. If a minor is traveling alone or with only one parent, authorities may ask for a notarized letter of consent from the non-traveling parent(s). This is something to think about if you're planning a family trip with younger travelers. Before you go, make sure to double-check the latest entry requirements, as they can change. I always find it helpful to check the Czech Republic's official consulate or embassy website in my country for the most up-to-date information. This is especially important in today's world, where rules around health or travel can shift unexpectedly.

Knowing these details ahead of time made my own travel experience much less stressful. With my documents in order and an understanding of what to expect, I was able to focus on enjoying the vibrant culture, rich history, and stunning architecture of the Czech Republic instead of worrying about logistics.

Health and Safety Updates

As I planned my journey to the Czech Republic, I prioritized understanding the health and safety measures to ensure a carefree and safe trip. Knowing that the Czech Republic boasts one of Europe's robust healthcare systems was reassuring. However, being prepared goes beyond acknowledging these facts; it's about understanding how they apply to a traveler like myself.

First, it's crucial to have comprehensive travel insurance. Although the Czech healthcare system is accessible to everyone, including tourists, having insurance means you're covered for everything from minor mishaps to major emergencies. I chose a policy that included coverage for medical expenses, trip cancellations, and any potential theft or loss. This is not just a safety net but a necessity, as it ensures you're not facing any high costs or complications while away from home. When it comes to public health, the

Czech Republic is vigilant, especially in cities like Prague, where the influx of tourists is significant. Vaccinations are not typically required for entry unless you're coming from an area with a risk of yellow fever. However, I made sure my routine vaccines, such as measles, mumps, and rubella (MMR), were up to date. Given the recent global health climate, checking for any specific health advisories before travel became a part of my routine preparation.

Safety in the Czech Republic is relatively straightforward. The crime rate against tourists is low, but like any major tourist destination, it's wise to be cautious of pickpocketing, especially in crowded areas such as the Charles Bridge or the Old Town Square. I always kept my belongings secure and maintained awareness of my surroundings, which is advice I'd give to any traveler. Moreover, Czech roads are well maintained, making driving a feasible option for exploring the countryside. However, I found the public transportation system in Prague and other cities exceptionally reliable and safe. It's affordable and efficient, and I used it frequently to navigate around without any issues. In terms of emergency services, knowing the number 112, which is the universal European emergency number, provided a layer of comfort. This number can be dialed for immediate assistance for police, medical services, or the fire department, and operators can respond in English, which is incredibly helpful in a stressful situation.

Lastly, understanding local customs and health regulations enhanced my travel experience. For instance, smoking is banned in all indoor dining areas, bars, and public buildings, which aligns with the country's commitment to public health. Additionally, tap water in the Czech Republic is safe to drink, which is great to know as a tourist looking to stay hydrated without constantly buying bottled water.

What to Pack: Prague Edition

When I first started packing for my trip to Prague, I was struck by the challenge of balancing comfort with style, especially given the city's varied landscape and weather patterns. Based on my experiences, here's a comprehensive rundown of what to bring to enjoy Prague without any hassles.

Footwear is perhaps the most crucial item on your packing list. Prague is a city best explored on foot, with endless cobblestone streets and hidden alleys that tell their own stories. Sturdy, comfortable walking shoes are a must, particularly ones that you've already broken in. I learned the hard way that new shoes and cobblestones don't mix well, after a couple of blisters. For evenings out, a pair of smarter shoes is advisable, as many upscale restaurants and clubs have a dress code. Clothing should be versatile and adaptable. Prague's weather can be quite unpredictable, swinging from sunny days to chilly evenings, regardless of the season. Layers are your best friend here. During my stay, I relied heavily on a combination of breathable fabrics for sunny days and warmer layers like sweaters and a lightweight, waterproof jacket for cooler evenings and rainy moments. Don't forget a stylish scarf or two, which can add a touch of elegance while keeping you warm.

Given Prague's vibrant cultural scene, you'll want to pack a few dressier options for attending performances at the National Theatre or enjoying a high-end dinner cruise on the Vltava River. A smart-casual outfit that can transition from day to night is perfect for this. Accessories should include a durable daypack or a crossbody bag to keep your essentials secure and hands-free as you roam. Prague is relatively safe, but like in any major city, it's wise to guard against pickpockets in crowded areas.

Tech gear should be travel-friendly. A good power bank, a universal adapter (the Czech Republic uses Type E and F plugs), and a good quality camera or smartphone are essential to capture the architectural beauty and vibrant street life of Prague. If you're planning to roam the city extensively, consider bringing a portable Wi-Fi device or ensuring your phone plan covers international data.

With these items packed, you'll be well-prepared to navigate the enchanting streets of Prague comfortably and stylishly. Packing right isn't just about having what you need; it's about making your travel experience as enjoyable and hassle-free as possible. From my first-hand experience, taking the time to pack thoughtfully for Prague allowed me to immerse fully in the rich history, vibrant culture, and breathtaking landscapes without any worries.

Budgeting for Your Trip: Expenses in Prague

Planning a budget for my trip to Prague was an essential part of the process, ensuring I could enjoy all the city has to offer without breaking the bank. Prague can be a paradise for visitors of all budgets, from the luxury seeker to the cost-conscious backpacker. Based on my experience, I discovered several ways to manage finances effectively, allowing for a rich experience in one of Europe's most picturesque cities.

Accommodation forms a significant part of any travel budget. In Prague, options vary widely. I found that staying a little outside the city center saved me a good deal of money. Hostels offer beds for as little as $10 a night, while mid-range hotels typically range from $60 to $100. For a more luxurious stay, five-star hotels can cost upwards of $200 per night. However, booking in advance and visiting in the shoulder season (early spring or late autumn) can lead to significant savings. Food and dining in Prague can be as economical or as lavish as you choose. Street food and local markets are budget-friendly options, with delicious items like trdelník (sweet pastry) and klobása (sausage) costing a few dollars. For dining out, an average meal at an inexpensive restaurant costs around $7-$15, while a three-course meal at a mid-range restaurant might set you back $20-$40 per person. Tipping is customary, usually around 10% of the bill, unless service is included.

Transportation costs are quite reasonable if you rely on public transport. Prague has an excellent system of trams, buses, and a metro, which can take you almost anywhere in the city. A short-term pass can be very cost-effective; for example, a 24-hour pass costs about $5, and a three-day pass is around $14. Taxis and rideshares are also available but can be more expensive, especially if you're navigating the city during peak traffic times. Sightseeing and entertainment expenses vary. Many of Prague's top attractions have entry fees, but purchasing a Prague Card can offer substantial savings. This tourist pass includes entry to over 60 attractions and unlimited public transport, priced around $70 for a two-day pass. Free activities abound as well—walking across the Charles Bridge, visiting Prague Castle's grounds, or enjoying the city's vibrant street performances can all be done without spending a penny.

Shopping in Prague can tempt any budget. From high-end boutiques to quirky souvenir shops, the choices are ample. I set aside a portion of my budget for shopping at local markets, where I picked up unique handmade crafts and art without overspending. By managing my budget according to these categories and planning ahead, I was able to enjoy a fulfilling trip to Prague without financial stress.

Optimal Travel Times

Choosing when to visit the Czech Republic was a crucial part of planning my trip, as each season dramatically shapes the travel experience. After much research and firsthand experience, I've gathered that the Czech Republic, with its continental climate, offers distinct and enchanting atmospheres throughout the year.

Spring (April to June) emerges as a favorite for many, including myself. This period marks a beautiful transformation as the cities and countryside alike burst into bloom. Prague in spring is particularly breathtaking with cherry blossoms adorning the streets and parks. The temperature is comfortably mild, ranging from 11°C to 20°C (52°F to 68°F), perfect for exploring historic sites and leisurely strolls through the winding streets without the bulk of heavy winter gear.

Summer (July to August) brings the warmest weather, with temperatures often climbing above 25°C (77°F). This is peak tourist season, and for good reason—long, sunny days make ideal conditions for sightseeing, outdoor dining, and participating in local festivals. However, it's also when Prague and other popular spots like Český Krumlov are most crowded. Despite the hustle, the vibrant atmosphere and the array of cultural events, from open-air concerts to traditional folk festivals, create a lively scene that's hard to resist.

Autumn (September to October) is my personal favorite time to visit. The summer crowds dissipate, and the scenery turns spectacularly golden. The weather remains gentle enough to enjoy outdoor activities, but with a crispness in the air that makes a cup of hot Czech coffee or a local brew even more enjoyable. It's also a great time to explore the vineyards of Moravia, as the grape harvest season brings a flurry of harvest festivals and wine tastings that showcase the region's rich viticultural heritage.

Winter (November to February) transforms the Czech Republic into a winter wonderland. While it can be quite cold, with temperatures often dipping below freezing, the festive spirit is palpable. Prague's Christmas markets are world-renowned; sipping mulled wine under the twinkling lights of the Old Town Square Market is a magical experience. For those who enjoy winter sports, the mountains offer excellent skiing and snowboarding conditions. Regardless of when you decide to visit, each season in the Czech Republic has its own charm and array of activities. For me, understanding these seasonal nuances was key to planning a trip that aligned with my interests and what I wanted to get out of the experience. Whether it's the spring blooms, summer festivals, autumnal harvest, or winter markets, the Czech Republic offers compelling reasons to visit year-round.

Understanding Local Culture and Social Norms

When I first planned my visit to the Czech Republic, I knew that immersing myself in the local culture and understanding the social norms would be essential to truly appreciate the experience. The Czech Republic, with its rich history and distinct cultural heritage, offers a tapestry of traditions and modern influences that can be quite enlightening for any traveler.

Initially, Czechs may appear reserved or formal, which reflects their polite nature. When meeting someone for the first time, it's customary to use formal greetings—using titles such as "Pan" (Mr.) or "Paní" (Mrs.) followed by the surname is standard. A firm handshake with direct eye contact is also appreciated. These formalities are often observed until a mutual agreement to switch to a first-name basis is made, which usually happens after some acquaintance. The Czechs appreciate direct communication but also value privacy and discretion. Small talk is not as common as in some other cultures; conversations tend to be straightforward and to the point. When discussing, it's important to be clear and concise, as this is seen as a sign of respect. However, humor, especially dry and subtle, is much cherished in personal conversations once the ice is broken. If you're invited to a Czech home, punctuality is essential as it's seen as a sign of respect. It's polite to bring a small gift, such as flowers, chocolates, or a bottle of wine. At the table, wait until the host invites you to start eating. Toasts are common, and you should look your fellow diners in the eyes when clinking glasses, saying "Na zdraví!" (To health!), which is the local way of saying cheers.

Czechs are generally quiet and reserved in public areas. Loud conversations or boisterous behavior on public transport or in restaurants are frowned upon. Respect for public spaces is significant, and keeping public areas clean and undisturbed is a practice deeply ingrained in the culture.

For everyday activities, Czechs tend to dress casually but neatly. However, for business or formal occasions, dressing smartly is expected. When visiting religious sites, appropriate attire should be worn as a sign of respect—this means covering shoulders and knees. In restaurants, it's customary to leave a tip, generally around 10-15% of the total bill, unless service was unsatisfactory. Tipping is also appreciated in taxis and for other services. It's customary to round up the amount to the nearest convenient number.

Throughout my journey, embracing these cultural nuances not only made my interactions smoother but also more genuine. I found that showing effort in respecting Czech traditions and social norms earned me warm smiles and an even warmer welcome.

Basic Czech Phrases for Travelers

Navigating the Czech Republic became significantly easier and more rewarding when I started to sprinkle some basic Czech phrases into my interactions. Even though many people in Prague and other tourist areas speak English, using Czech phrases really enriched my experiences and often brought a smile to the locals' faces. Here are some fundamental Czech phrases that I found essential for any traveler.

Greetings

- Dobrý den (DOH-bree dehn) - "Good day" or "Hello," used from morning until late afternoon. It's the most common greeting and is appropriate in almost all situations.
- Dobré ráno (DOH-breh RAH-no) - "Good morning," typically used before noon.
- Dobrý večer (DOH-bree VEH-chair) - "Good evening," used in the later part of the day.

Basic Politeness

- Prosím (PRO-seem) - This versatile word can mean "please," "here you go," or "can I help you?" depending on the context.
- Děkuji (DYEH-koo-yee) - "Thank you." It's crucial to show gratitude, and locals appreciate when you do.
- Promiňte (PRO-meen-teh) or Pardon - "Excuse me," used to get someone's attention or to apologize in a minor incident.
- Ano (AH-no) - "Yes."
- Ne (neh) - "No."

At a Restaurant or Café:

- Můžu dostat menu, prosím? (MOO-zhoo DOH-stat MEH-noo PRO-seem?) - "Can I get a menu, please?"
- Můžu zaplatit, prosím? (MOO-zhoo ZAP-la-teet PRO-seem?) - "Can I pay, please?"

- Chtěl bych kávu (khtyel bih KA-voo) - "I would like coffee."
- S mlékem, prosím (s MLYEH-kem PRO-seem) - "With milk, please."

Asking for Directions
- Kde je...? (Kdeh yeh...?) - "Where is...?"
- Toalety (TOH-ah-leh-tee) - "Restrooms."
- Nádraží (NAH-drah-zhi) - "Train station."
- Nemocnice (neh-MOHTS-nee-tseh) - "Hospital."

Emergencies
- Pomoc! (POH-mohts) - "Help!"
- Zavolejte policii! (ZAH-voh-lyeht-teh poh-LEE-tsee) - "Call the police!"

These phrases were not just tools for communication; they were keys to unlocking a more authentic and interactive travel experience. Each time I used them, I could see the respect and appreciation in the eyes of the locals, making each conversation more engaging and meaningful. Learning these phrases also showed me the importance of cultural respect, which is crucial when visiting another country.

Remember, pronunciation can be tricky, but don't be afraid to try—locals usually appreciate your effort regardless of mistakes. Carrying a small phrasebook or having a translation app handy can also boost your confidence and ensure you're never truly lost for words.

CHAPTER 2

Arrival and Transportation

Arriving in Prague, the heart of Central Europe, sets the stage for a seamless and picturesque entry into a city that perfectly blends ancient charm with modern efficiency. From the moment you step off the plane or train, the transport options available make navigating this beautiful city a breeze. Whether you arrive at Václav Havel Airport or one of the main railway stations, you are well-positioned to dive straight into your Prague adventure.

Václav Havel Airport, located just a few kilometers from the city center, offers numerous links into the heart of Prague. You can choose from a variety of transport methods such as buses, shuttles, and taxis, each providing a comfortable and efficient route to your destination. The integration of these services with Prague's public transport system ensures that you can reach downtown smoothly and start exploring without delay. For those arriving by train, Prague's main railway stations, including the bustling Praha Hlavní Nádraží, serve as grand gateways into the city's vibrant life. Here, the transition from traveler to tourist is made simple with straightforward connections to trams, buses, and the metro. These stations are not just transit points but also part of the city's historic and architectural heritage, making your arrival an instant immersion into Czech culture.

Once in the city, navigating Prague is an experience in itself. The public transport network is renowned for its reliability and coverage, with trams, buses, and a metro system that reach every corner of the city. For those who prefer to explore at their own pace, renting a bike or simply walking through the compact city center offers a more personal view of Prague's picturesque streets and stunning landmarks.

In this chapter, we'll explore all these options in detail, giving you all the information you need to choose the best way to arrive and travel around Prague. Whether you prefer the speed and convenience of the metro or the scenic routes taken by trams and buses, understanding Prague's transport essentials will undoubtedly enhance your visit.

Arriving in Prague: Air and Rail Options

Arriving in Prague by air is a smooth and welcoming experience, thanks to Václav Havel Airport Prague, which is situated about 15 kilometers west of the city center. Named after the former president, this airport is not only the largest in the Czech Republic but also among the busiest in Central Europe. It serves as a hub connecting various international and domestic flights, making it an accessible point for travelers from across the globe.

When I arrived, I was impressed by the airport's modern facilities and the efficiency of the services. From the moment you land, you can choose from multiple transportation options to reach the city center. The most economical is the public bus. Bus routes 100 and 119 connect to different metro lines: route 100 to Metro Line B at Zličín and route 119 to Metro Line A at Nádraží Veleslavín. Each ride to the metro station takes about 15-20 minutes, and from there, the city center is just a few metro stops away. For those preferring a direct route, the Airport Express bus heads straight to the main train station, Hlavní nádraží, which is centrally located and convenient for those carrying heavier luggage or preferring less transit.

Alternatively, taxis and rideshare services like Uber are readily available. A taxi ride to the city center is typically a 25-minute journey, depending on traffic, and can cost around 500-700 CZK. Always ensure that the taxi is reputable—look for the official taxi signage—and that the meter is running, or agree on a fare beforehand to avoid any surprises. For those arriving by rail, Prague is equally well-connected. The city's main railway station, Praha Hlavní nádraží, is an architectural marvel in itself and serves as a central hub for domestic and international trains. This station links Prague with major European cities via frequent and reliable services. I arrived here from

Berlin and found the onward connections to the metro (Line C) and trams straightforward. The station is just a short walk from Wenceslas Square and the heart of Prague's New Town.

Rail travel offers a scenic and relaxed alternative to flying, with services like EuroCity and InterCity providing efficient connections. Trains are spacious, offering both second and first-class accommodations, and you'll find that traveling through the rolling landscapes of the Czech countryside is a visually rewarding experience.

No matter how you arrive, Prague welcomes you with open arms, offering a blend of historical charm and modern convenience. My arrival felt like stepping back in time yet with all the comforts of modern infrastructure, setting the stage for a memorable visit.

Navigating Prague: Public Transport and Other Means

Navigating Prague was one of the highlights of my visit, thanks to its superbly organized and efficient public transport system. From the moment I stepped out of the hotel, I found myself marveling at how easy and convenient it was to explore this historic city using a variety of transit options.

Prague's Metro system is a lifeline for both locals and tourists. It consists of three lines—A (green), B (yellow), and C (red)—that connect major parts of the city. The metro stations are well-marked, making them easy to find and use. I particularly appreciated the cleanliness and the frequency of the trains; during peak hours, they run every 2-3 minutes, which means I never had to wait long. The metro operates from early morning until midnight, which covered most of my needs.

The tram network in Prague is not only functional but also a wonderful way to see the city. Many tram routes pass through scenic areas, offering a lovely view from the comfort of your seat. The tram system is especially useful for reaching places that are not accessible by the metro, such as the picturesque Prague Castle. Trams run frequently and until late, with night trams ensuring connectivity even after midnight.

While I used buses less frequently, they are crucial for reaching certain suburban areas of Prague and locations like the airport. The buses maintain a tight schedule, are clean, and are equipped with electronic boards that announce upcoming stops, which is helpful for someone unfamiliar with the language.

One of the best aspects of Prague's public transport is the ticketing system. A single ticket can be used across metros, trams, and buses. Tickets are time-based, with options ranging from

30 minutes up to several days, which is ideal for tourists. I bought a 3-day pass that allowed unlimited travel, and it was incredibly cost-effective and convenient, eliminating the need to purchase individual tickets for each journey.

Beyond public transport, walking around Prague is a joy. The city center is compact and studded with cafes, shops, and historical sites, making it very pedestrian-friendly. For longer distances, I tried the city's bike-sharing system. It's easy to rent a bike using an app, and cycling along the Vltava River was both refreshing and exhilarating.

For late nights or when I was laden with shopping bags, I opted for taxis or ride-sharing services. They are readily available, but it's advisable to use a reliable taxi service or a well-known ride-sharing app to ensure fair pricing and safety.

CHAPTER 3

Where to Stay

Deciding where to stay in Prague was one of the most exciting parts of planning my trip. The city offers a diverse array of accommodations that cater to every possible preference and budget, each adding its unique flavor to my stay. From luxurious hotels to quaint boutique inns, ski resorts, historical lodgings, family-friendly options, and even agritourism sites, Prague truly has something for everyone.

Luxury accommodations in Prague are not just places to sleep, but are experiences in themselves. I found myself enamored by hotels that not only provided opulent comfort but also boasted rich histories and stunning views of the city's iconic skyline. On the other end of the spectrum, budget-friendly options offered clean, efficient, and modern amenities without the frills, proving that comfort doesn't have to come at a high price.

For a more personalized touch, the characteristic boutique inns scattered across Prague's cobblestoned streets offered a warm welcome with their unique themes and intimate settings. Each inn presented an opportunity to dive deeper into the local culture and history, making my stay as educational as it was relaxing. Exploring the city in the winter, I was also drawn to the ski resorts just outside Prague, which provided a perfect blend of adventure and tranquility away from the bustling city center. Meanwhile, the historical lodgings in ancient buildings whisked me back in time, allowing me to live like a local in centuries-old surroundings.

For those traveling with family, Prague's family-friendly hotels and vacation stays ensured that guests of all ages felt comfortable and entertained. And for a truly unique experience, staying at one of the heritage properties or agritourism sites allowed me to appreciate the Czech Republic's natural beauty and rural traditions.

Additionally, navigating the reservation process was made easy through preferred booking platforms that offered transparent reviews and competitive prices, helping me make informed decisions about where to stay based on reliable feedback from fellow travelers.

Each type of accommodation in Prague offered its own set of benefits and experiences, making it clear that where you choose to stay can deeply influence how you experience this magnificent city. This chapter will explore these options in detail, providing insights to help you find the perfect home away from home in Prague.

Accommodation Ranges: Luxury to Economical

During my travels in the Czech Republic, I discovered a delightful spectrum of accommodation options catering to various budget levels, from the opulently luxurious to the comfortably economical. Here's an overview that blends my personal insights with practical information to help you choose the right place to stay.

For those looking to indulge in luxury, Prague and other Czech cities offer some world-class hotels that combine history with lavish modern comforts.

1. **The Four Seasons Hotel Prague**
   - **Location:** Veleslavínova 2a/1098, 110 00 Staré Město, Czechia
   - **Contact:** +420 221 427 000 | website: www.fourseasons.com/prague
   - **Price Range:** $350 - $700 per night

- **Amenities:** This hotel provides stunning views of the Vltava River and Prague Castle, an on-site spa, gourmet dining, and sumptuously appointed rooms. It's ideally located near the Charles Bridge, making it a perfect spot from which to explore the city's historic sites.

2. Alchymist Grand Hotel and Spa

- **Location:** Tržiště 19, 118 00 Malá Strana, Czechia
- **Contact:** +420 257 286 011 | email: info@alchymisthotel.com
- **Price Range:** $250 - $500 per night
- **Amenities:** Set in a magnificent Baroque building, the hotel offers a luxurious spa, indoor pool, and an enchanting garden. Guests can enjoy a truly opulent setting with antique furnishings and top-notch service.

For travelers seeking a balance between cost and comfort, mid-range hotels offer excellent services without the luxury price tag.

1. Hotel Pod Věží

- **Location:** Mostecká 58/2, 118 00 Malá Strana, Czechia
- **Contact:** +420 257 532 041 | website: www.podvezi.com
- **Price Range:** $100 - $200 per night
- **Amenities:** Located right next to the Charles Bridge, this hotel provides cozy, clean rooms with fantastic service. The location is unbeatable for sightseeing and exploring Prague's old town.

2. Design Hotel Jewel Prague

- **Location:** Rytířská 3, 110 00 Nové Město, Czechia
- **Contact:** +420 775 422 111 | email: info@hoteljewelprague.com
- **Price Range:** $90 - $150 per night

- **Amenities:** A small boutique hotel with stylish rooms, personalized service, and a delightful breakfast served in a quaint café setting. It's a gem in the heart of Prague for those who appreciate attention to detail.

Budget-conscious travelers can also find comfortable stays without sacrificing cleanliness or location.

1. Czech Inn

- **Location:** Francouzská 76, 101 00 Vinohrady, Czechia
- **Contact:** +420 267 267 600 | website: www.czech-inn.com
- **Price Range:** $20 - $50 per night
- **Amenities:** As part of the famous Europe's Famous Hostels, Czech Inn offers modern design, clean facilities, and a friendly environment. It's popular among young

travelers and provides options from dorm beds to private rooms.

2. Hostel Downtown

- **Location:** Narodni 19, 110 00 Nové Město, Czechia
- **Contact:** +420 224 240 879 | email: info@hosteldowntown.cz
- **Price Range:** $15 - $40 per night
- **Amenities:** This hostel is known for its lively atmosphere and friendly staff. They offer both dormitory-style and private rooms, plus organized activities like walking tours and cooking nights which are great for meeting other travelers.

Each of these options reflects the diversity and accessibility of accommodations in the Czech Republic, providing a range from the height of luxury to practical economy. Choosing where to stay will depend on your personal preferences, budget, and the type of experience you wish to have while visiting this captivating country.

Characteristic Boutique Inns and Historical Lodgings

As I ventured through the Czech Republic, I was captivated by the charm and distinctive character of the accommodations available. From the cobblestone streets of Prague to the serene landscapes of the countryside, the variety of places to stay added layers of depth to my travel experience.

In Prague, boutique inns are a special treat, offering personalized experiences and a taste of local hospitality. One such gem is the Miss Sophie's Hotel, nestled in the New Town at Melounova 3, 120 00 Prague 2. This inn blends modern design with classic elements, providing a cozy, intimate atmosphere that feels both upscale and welcoming. Each room is uniquely decorated, reflecting aspects of Czech culture and art. Getting there is easy with a short tram ride from the central station, which drops you off just a few minutes' walk from the inn.

For those intrigued by history, staying in a historical lodging can be like traveling back in time. The Chateau Mcely, for example, is an exquisite option. This restored castle, located in Mcely, about an hour's drive from Prague, is steeped in history and luxury. It offers guests a chance to stay in opulently restored rooms that capture the essence of Czech aristocracy. The castle is not just a place to stay but an experience, with its spa, gourmet restaurant, and the surrounding forest that invites exploration.

Each of these accommodations—boutique inns and historical lodgings—provides more than just a place to sleep; they offer a gateway into the culture and history of the Czech Republic. Whether you're waking up in a luxurious room in a historical castle or enjoying a bespoke cocktail in a chic inn, these places enrich your travel experience with their unique stories and settings. They are easily accessible by public transport or car rentals from major cities, ensuring that wherever you choose to stay, you remain connected to the rest of the country's sights and experiences.

This journey through the Czech Republic's diverse accommodations not only provided comfort but also deepened my understanding and appreciation of this beautiful country, making each moment of my stay as enriching as the destinations I explored.

Family-Friendly Hotels and Vacation Stays

Traveling with family requires special consideration, especially when it comes to finding the right place to stay. During my visit to the Czech Republic, I was on the lookout for accommodations that would cater not just to adults but also be delightful for children. Thankfully, the Czech Republic offers a plethora of family-friendly options that combine comfort with convenience and ensure that all family members have a memorable stay.

Aquapalace Hotel Prague

- **Location:** Pražská 137, Čestlice 251 01, Czech Republic
- **Contact:** +420 225 108 888 | info@aquapalacehotel.cz
- **Website:**(https://www.aquapalacehotel.cz/en)
- **Price Range:** $100 - $200 per night

- **Amenities:** This hotel is part of the larger Aquapalace Praha, the largest water park in Central Europe. The hotel itself offers family rooms and suites, a spa, and wellness area, and direct access to the water park, which is a hit with kids and adults alike. It's an excellent choice for families looking for fun and relaxation in one place. The location is just a short drive from Prague, providing a peaceful retreat with easy city access.

Falkensteiner Hotel Maria Prag

- **Location:** Opletalova 1402/21, 110 00 Nové Město, Czech Republic
- **Contact:** +420 222 211 229 | info.mariaprag@falkensteiner.com
- **Website:**(https://www.falkensteiner.com/en/hotel/maria-prag)
- **Price Range:** $120 - $250 per night
- **Amenities:** Located in the heart of Prague, this hotel is perfect for families who want

to explore the city. It offers spacious family rooms, a children's program, and amenities like baby monitors and bottle warmers on request. The proximity to major attractions like the Old Town Square and the Charles Bridge makes it an ideal base for sightseeing.

Hotel Grandium
- **Location:** Politických vězňů 913/12, 110 00 Nové Město, Czech Republic
- **Contact:** +420 234 100 100 | reservation@hotelgrandium.cz
- **Website:**(https://www.hotelgrandium.cz/en)
- **Price Range:** $80 - $180 per night
- **Amenities:** With its central location near Wenceslas Square, the Hotel Grandium offers a family-friendly atmosphere with modern amenities. They provide family rooms, a kid-friendly buffet, and

assistance with arranging tickets to local attractions and public transport.

Penzion Bílý Beránek

- **Location:** Hradčany, 48, 543 71 Hostinné, Czech Republic
- **Contact:** +420 499 441 534 | info@bilyberanek.cz
- **Website:** (https://www.bilyberanek.cz/)
- **Price Range:** $50 - $100 per night
- **Amenities:** This charming guesthouse is located in a quieter part of the country, making it perfect for families looking to experience the Czech countryside. They offer spacious family rooms, a playground for children, and outdoor activities such as hiking and cycling. The family-friendly atmosphere extends to their dining options, with special menus for younger guests.

Distinctive Stays: Heritage Properties and Agritourism Sites

When you think of a getaway in the Czech Republic, you might immediately picture Prague's medieval charm or the buzz of the larger cities. But the country is also home to a wealth of distinctive stays that transport you back in time, offering a unique blend of history, tradition, and the Czech countryside. Heritage properties and agritourism sites are increasingly popular for travelers looking for more than just a bed to sleep in—they want an experience. After spending some time exploring these kinds of stays, I can tell you there's no better way to truly feel the pulse of Czech culture.

Heritage properties in the Czech Republic come in many shapes and sizes. These include everything from restored castles and manor houses to traditional, family-run hotels tucked away in small villages. One of my favorites has to be the Chateau Herálec, located about 90 minutes southeast of Prague, in the Vysočina region. This 17th-century Baroque castle has been meticulously renovated into a luxurious hotel while retaining much of its original charm. Expect to step into a world where antique furniture, chandeliers, and crystal glassware greet you at every turn. A night here will set you back around $150 to $300 per night, depending on the season and room selection. You can reach the chateau via a direct train from Prague to the nearby town of Havlíčkův Brod, followed by a short taxi ride.

For something closer to the heart of the city, Hotel U Tri Pstrosu in Prague is another gem. While this property isn't exactly a castle, it boasts a history dating back to the 14th century, with plenty of medieval flair. The hotel is located in the Old Town, near the Astronomical Clock, and offers an intimate, historical experience at a much more reasonable price. Rooms here can range from $80 to $150 a night, and its proximity to major attractions like the Charles Bridge and Old Town

Square make it a favorite for tourists who want to stay somewhere with rich character and a central location. The hotel is easily accessible by tram or metro, with the nearest station being Staroměstská.

On the other hand, if you're craving an authentic rural experience, agritourism sites in the Czech Republic are a must-try. These places offer a real taste of Czech farm life, where you can learn about traditional farming methods, help out with animal care, or simply enjoy a hearty farm-to-table meal. One particularly special agritourism stay is Penzion U Horských Farmářů, located in the Jeseníky mountains. This family-run pension offers comfortable, rustic rooms with beautiful views of the surrounding hills. Prices here range from $70 to $150 per night, and guests can enjoy homemade Czech meals made with fresh, local ingredients. It's an easy drive from Olomouc, about 2 hours from Prague, or a 3-hour bus ride from Brno.

If you're looking for a truly unique experience, you might also want to explore the Statek U Sněhurky, a farmstay located in the heart of the Bohemian countryside. This one is particularly great for families, with activities like apple picking, bread-making, and the chance to help out with farm chores. The property is also very focused on sustainability, with eco-friendly practices that make it an ideal choice for those interested in green travel. Rates here range from $60 to $120 a night, and you can reach it via a short taxi ride from the nearby town of Mělník, which is accessible by train from Prague.

Both heritage properties and agritourism stays in the Czech Republic offer more than just a place to lay your head—they offer a chance to step into another world. Whether you're in a stately manor, a medieval hotel, or a rural farmhouse, you'll get a deeper connection to Czech culture and history than any standard hotel could offer.

Reservation Insights and Preferred Booking Platforms

When I first started planning my trip to the Czech Republic, I quickly realized that understanding how to make the right reservations was just as important as picking the destinations themselves. Booking accommodations, tours, and experiences in a country with so much history and so many hidden gems can be tricky, especially if you're unfamiliar with the local booking platforms and the specific nuances of Czech travel. After a few trips and plenty of trial and error, I've found a few insights and strategies that make the booking process smoother, and I'm excited to share them.

First, it's worth noting that most travelers, including myself, usually prefer to book accommodations well in advance, especially during peak seasons like spring and fall. The Czech Republic, with its stunning castles, charming towns, and beautiful countryside, can get busy, so it's best to secure your spot early.

While traditional methods, like calling a hotel directly, can sometimes be useful, I've found that booking through platforms like Booking.com, Hotels.com, and AirBnB often offers more convenience and flexibility. These platforms are well-established and reliable, with most properties listed in English and a range of prices to suit different budgets.

Booking.com is perhaps the most straightforward option, especially for those of us who are used to booking stays in other European destinations. The platform allows for easy filtering by location, price range, and amenities, which can be especially helpful if you're looking for something specific like family-friendly stays or historical properties. One of the things I've appreciated most is the cancellation policy. Many accommodations on Booking.com offer free cancellation up to 24 hours before your stay, which provides peace of mind, particularly when travel plans sometimes change unexpectedly. In terms of pricing, you can expect to pay anywhere from $50 to $300 a night depending on the type of accommodation you're booking—be it a budget-friendly guesthouse or a more luxurious historical hotel.

For a more immersive, locally focused experience, I recommend trying platforms like CzechTourism, which is the official site for the Czech Republic's national tourism. This platform not only lists accommodation options but also provides insight into smaller, locally-run places, including agritourism sites and boutique hotels that you might not find on larger, international booking platforms. This site also features detailed descriptions and real-time availability, which is key for planning a trip around lesser-known destinations like rural villages in Moravia or small towns in Bohemia. Prices vary here as well, but for unique stays, you might find rates between $40 and $150 a night.

If you're looking for something unique—say, a stay in a renovated Czech chateau or a farmhouse on a vineyard—Airbnb is another excellent platform. It's a personal favorite for finding properties with character. I've stayed in a few beautifully restored homes on the outskirts of Prague, where the host's personal touch made the stay feel special. The range of prices here is huge, from $50 for a simple apartment to $250 or more for a private villa or historic property. The advantage of using Airbnb is that you often get to interact with local hosts who are full of insights into the area, and the listings usually feature a lot of user reviews, which can help with decision-making.

But booking accommodation isn't just about picking the right platform—it's also about knowing when to book and how to handle cancellations. I've learned that if you plan on visiting during the high season (April to October), booking at least 3–6 weeks in advance is a safe bet. Hotels and guesthouses near popular destinations like Prague and Český Krumlov can fill up quickly. If you're traveling during off-peak seasons, you can often get away with booking closer to your arrival date, but remember that weekends in smaller towns can still be busy, especially if there are any local festivals or events.

A great tip I picked up during my trips is to always keep an eye out for deals on accommodation packages. Some platforms, like Expedia, offer bundled deals where you can get discounted rates for booking flights and accommodation together. These can be quite helpful if you're flying into the country and looking to book a longer stay. While you can sometimes get a better deal by booking directly through the hotel or property's website, booking platforms often provide perks like loyalty points or discounts for future stays, which can add up to big savings over time.

For tours and excursions, I've found Viator and GetYourGuide to be excellent resources for booking activities in advance. Whether you're looking for a guided tour of Prague Castle or a day trip to the picturesque town of Kutná Hora, these platforms provide a range of options, including skip-the-line tickets, which can save you hours of waiting. I've personally used them to book everything from cooking classes to historical walking tours, and the experience has always been seamless. Prices here can range from $30 for a local half-day tour to $150 for more specialized, full-day experiences.

So, while the process of booking stays in the Czech Republic can feel a bit overwhelming at first, with the right resources and a bit of planning, it becomes a smooth and enjoyable part of the trip. Platforms like Booking.com, Airbnb, and CzechTourism offer a diverse range of choices to suit every type of traveler, from those seeking luxury to those looking for local, off-the-beaten-path gems. The key is to book early if you're traveling during peak times, to always check for cancellation policies, and to keep your eyes peeled for package deals that might offer savings across the board. Trust me, once you've mastered the booking process, everything else in your Czech adventure will fall into place.

CHAPTER 4

Food and Dining

When I first visited the Czech Republic, one of the things that stood out to me the most was the food. I had heard the rumors—hearty, satisfying, and rich in history—but nothing quite prepared me for the depth of flavors I would encounter. From the moment I sat down at a local tavern in Prague, the Czech culinary experience felt like a warm embrace. Whether it was the dense, flavorful bread dumplings paired with slow-braised pork, or the sweet, syrupy goodness of Trdelník being prepared fresh on the streets, each bite was a new discovery. But Czech cuisine isn't just about the food itself—it's a reflection of centuries-old traditions, influenced by the region's agricultural landscape and its diverse history.

In this chapter, I'll walk you through the Czech food scene as I've come to experience it. I'll introduce you to some traditional dishes you absolutely have to try—those hearty, rustic meals that form the backbone of Czech comfort food. Alongside these, I'll share some of Prague's best dining spots, where you can savor local flavors in both casual and upscale settings. If you're a vegetarian or vegan, don't worry—there's plenty to explore, too. The food scene in the Czech Republic is evolving, and there are great options for plant-based eaters as well. I'll also point you to some of the best cafes and bistros in the city, where you can pause and enjoy a cup of coffee, a slice of cake, or even a quick snack.

For those of you who want to get your hands dirty (literally and figuratively), I'll also recommend some of the top culinary courses and food tours in the country. These experiences are a great way to learn more about Czech cooking techniques, the culture behind the dishes, and the ingredients that make this cuisine so unique.

Traditional Czech Dishes to Try

During my time in the Czech Republic, I quickly realized that the country's food culture is built around comfort, tradition, and hearty ingredients that reflect its long history and diverse regions. Every dish I encountered felt like a small window into the Czech way of life—uncomplicated, satisfying, and steeped in centuries of tradition. If you're planning a trip, there are certain dishes you simply cannot miss, so let me walk you through some of the most iconic Czech foods you should try.

One of the first dishes I couldn't resist trying was Svíčková, a rich and creamy beef dish that is quintessentially Czech. It's made from beef tenderloin that's slowly simmered in a velvety sauce of carrots, onions, cream, and a hint of vinegar. This dish is often served with the famous knedlíky (Czech dumplings)—soft, pillowy bread dumplings that soak up the sauce beautifully. It's the perfect meal for a chilly evening in Prague, and I found it to be incredibly comforting, especially when paired with a cold Czech pilsner.

If you're looking for something a bit more rustic, vepřo knedlo zelo is another must-try. This dish is a true celebration of Czech flavors: roast pork, sauerkraut, and those same soft dumplings I mentioned earlier. It's simple, but the slow-roasted pork has a wonderful, crisp exterior while staying juicy on the inside. The sauerkraut adds a tangy contrast to the richness of the meat, and the whole plate comes together as a perfect example of Czech home-cooked food. This dish can be found all over the country, from family-run taverns in the countryside to upscale restaurants in Prague.

Another classic you should not overlook is goulash, a hearty stew that, while originating in Hungary, has become a favorite in the Czech Republic. Czech goulash is typically made with beef, onions, and paprika, giving it a robust and flavorful broth. It's often served with bread dumplings or a slice of fresh bread to mop up the sauce. The dish is so beloved that you'll find it on nearly every restaurant menu, and each version offers its own little twist, though they all retain that deep, comforting flavor.

If you're in the mood for something lighter, koleno (roast pig's knee) is a classic Czech beer hall dish. It's exactly as it sounds: a large, slow-roasted piece of pig's knee, often accompanied by mustard, horseradish, and a hearty bread. The skin is crisped up perfectly, and the meat itself is tender and juicy. It's typically served as a shared dish, making it a perfect choice for a social meal with friends or family.

And then there's Trdelník, which, although not originally Czech, has become a beloved street food in Prague and beyond. It's a sweet pastry, often rolled in sugar and walnuts, and cooked on a rotating spit until golden and crispy. You'll see it sold at markets and street stalls, especially around the holidays. It's warm, sweet, and incredibly satisfying—perfect for a quick snack as you explore the winding streets of Prague.

Don't forget to sample the Czech soups, which are an essential part of any meal. One of the most famous is česnečka, a garlicky soup that's often served as a remedy after a long night out. It's made with a rich broth, plenty of garlic, and sometimes served with croutons or cheese. It's simple but packs a punch, and it's the kind of dish that feels like a warm hug on a cold day.

For dessert, I was drawn to koláče, a traditional Czech pastry filled with fruit, poppy seeds, or sweet cheese. It's a versatile sweet treat that can be found at bakeries and cafes across the country, and each region puts its own spin on it. I found the plum-filled ones to be especially delicious, with the sweet, tart fruit perfectly complementing the buttery dough.

Finally, let's talk about Czech beer. It's a culture in itself here, and the country is known for having some of the best beer in the world. Pilsner Urquell is the most famous, but there are countless local breweries with their own unique brews. It's common to see locals enjoying a glass of cold lager with almost every meal, and as a visitor, it's easy to get caught up in the tradition. Whether you're at a historic pub or a modern bar, the Czech love affair with beer is something you'll want to be a part of.

From savory dishes to sweet pastries, the Czech Republic offers a food experience that feels both rooted in history and open to new ideas. The next time you're in the country, I encourage you to dive deep into these traditional flavors and explore what makes Czech cuisine so special. Trust me, every bite will tell you a story of the country's past and its vibrant present.

Premier Dining Spots in Prague

When I first set foot in Prague, I quickly realized that its culinary scene isn't just about hearty traditional fare—although that's certainly part of it. This city offers a wide range of premier dining spots that serve as an exciting intersection of Czech history, modern innovation, and international flavors. Whether you're looking for a Michelin-star experience or a sleek contemporary restaurant offering seasonal, locally sourced ingredients, Prague's fine dining scene is rich, diverse, and full of hidden gems. If you're a food lover like me, here are some of the best places to sit down for an unforgettable meal.

One of my absolute favorite spots is La Degustation Bohême Bourgeoise. This Michelin-starred restaurant is not only about exquisite food but also about immersing yourself in Czech history through the lens of modern gastronomy. Located in the heart of Prague, at Haštalská 18, 110 00 Praha 1, La Degustation offers an intimate and creative dining experience with a seasonal tasting menu that reinterprets classic Czech dishes. The tasting menu can range from $90 to $140 per person, depending on your choice of wine pairings. The staff is exceptionally knowledgeable, and the ambiance is sophisticated yet warm, making it the perfect place for a special evening. If you love refined, thought-provoking dishes and a personalized dining experience, this place is a must-visit. For reservations or inquiries, you can reach them at +420 222 320 000 or visit their website (http://www.ladegustation.cz).

For something equally special, yet a bit more relaxed, Field Restaurant is another incredible choice. This Michelin-starred gem is located at U Milosrdných 3, 110 00 Praha 1 and is known for its minimalist, modern aesthetic and creative, vegetable-forward cuisine. The chefs at Field focus on using seasonal ingredients in inventive ways, with dishes that surprise and delight in both flavor and presentation. The tasting menu, which can also be paired with wine, is priced between $80 and $120. Whether you're a meat lover or a vegetarian, the dishes here are beautifully composed and full of vibrant flavors. The service is exceptional, and the ambiance is sophisticated but not intimidating. To book a table, visit their website at (http://www.fieldrestaurant.cz) or call them at +420 224 937 373.

If you're looking for an unforgettable dining experience in a historic setting, V Zátiší is a premier choice. Situated at U Lužického semináře 7, 118 00 Praha 1, V Zátiší is one of the city's longest-running fine dining restaurants. Here, you'll find a creative blend of Czech and international flavors, all served in a cozy, elegant environment. The restaurant has been around for decades, yet it constantly reinvents itself with a focus on contemporary, seasonal dishes. Prices here typically range from $40 to $80 per person for a three-course meal, and they also offer exceptional wine pairings. The atmosphere is elegant, perfect for a romantic dinner or a celebration. You can make reservations by calling +420 257 532 732 or visiting (http://www.vzatisi.cz).

Another exceptional choice for those seeking premium dining is Café Savoy, located at Vítězná 5, 150 00 Praha 5. While it's more of a café than a restaurant, Café Savoy offers a fantastic blend of Czech and European fare in a beautifully restored space that feels like you've stepped back in time. The high ceilings and grand design make it an elegant place to enjoy breakfast, brunch, or a light lunch. Their breakfast menu is one of the best I've ever had, with options ranging from traditional Czech pastries to more international dishes. Expect to pay around $15 to $30 for a full breakfast or lunch. For more information, visit their website at (http://www.cafesavoy.cz) or call +420 257 532 306.

For those who love sushi and modern Asian fusion, Maitrea is an unexpected treasure right in the city center at Týnská 6, 110 00 Praha 1. While Prague is known for its hearty meats and dumplings, Maitrea brings a refreshing change with its Asian-inspired menu, blending flavors from Japan, Thailand, and other regions. This place has a Zen-like atmosphere, with its calm, minimalist design offering a perfect escape from the hustle and bustle of Prague's streets. Expect to pay around $25 to $50 for a satisfying meal, with some standout dishes like the tuna tataki and miso soup. To make a reservation or inquire further, check out their website (http://www.maitrea.cz) or call +420 222 221 759.

And if you're in the mood for Italian food, CottoCrudo at the Four Seasons Hotel Prague(at Veleslavínova 2a, 110 00 Praha 1) offers one of the most refined dining experiences in the city. With its chic, contemporary design and sweeping views of the Vltava River, this Italian restaurant serves up delicious pastas, seafood, and hand-crafted pizzas that transport you straight to Italy. The service here is impeccable, and the atmosphere is both chic and laid-back. Expect to pay around $50 to $80 per person, depending on the wine and courses you choose. To book a table, visit their website at (https://www.fourseasons.com/prague/dining/cott ocrudo) or call +420 221 427 000.

When dining out in Prague, you're never far from incredible culinary experiences that blend tradition and modern innovation. Each of these premier dining spots offers something unique, whether it's Michelin-star excellence, a stunning atmosphere, or exceptional food quality. So, no matter where you end up, you're bound to have a meal you'll remember for years to come. Whether you're looking for fine dining or simply a place to enjoy a leisurely lunch, Prague's best restaurants have something to offer every palate and every occasion.

Best Restaurants for Local Flavors

When you visit the Czech Republic, it's not just the stunning architecture or charming cobblestone streets that leave an impression—it's the food. Czech cuisine is hearty, satisfying, and full of rich flavors that reflect the country's history and culture. During my own travels, I discovered that some of the best ways to experience the true essence of Czech life is by diving into the local culinary scene. If you're eager to savor authentic Czech flavors, here are some of the best restaurants where you can enjoy traditional dishes, lovingly prepared with fresh, local ingredients.

One of the best places to start your culinary adventure in Prague is U Modré Kachničky. Tucked away at Nebovidská 6, 118 00 Praha 1, this charming restaurant specializes in traditional Czech game meat dishes, including duck, venison, and wild boar. The rustic, cozy atmosphere makes it the perfect place to enjoy a hearty meal. The menu is full of dishes that are staples of Czech cuisine, with a modern twist. I tried their famous duck with braised cabbage and dumplings, and it was absolutely delicious—crispy on the outside and tender on the inside, with just the right amount of seasoning. Expect to pay between $25 to $45 per person for a main course, and if you're feeling adventurous, try one of their regional wine pairings. For more information or reservations, visit (http://www.umodrekachnicky.cz) or call +420 257 533 814.

Another gem in the city is Lokál. Located at Dlouhá 33, 110 00 Praha 1, Lokál is a favorite among locals and visitors alike for its authentic Czech pub experience. This bustling, no-frills eatery focuses on hearty, traditional Czech dishes like svíčková (marinated beef in creamy sauce) and pilsner schnitzel, paired with some of the best draft beers in the city. The food here is simple yet flavorful, and the portions are generous, making it perfect for those looking to fill up after a day of sightseeing. I've visited Lokál a few times, and I always find the koleno (braised pork knee) to be a standout dish—tender, juicy, and served with mustard and pickles. You can expect to spend around $15 to $25 for a meal here. It's a great place to feel the pulse of Czech dining and enjoy some hearty comfort food. For more details, check out their website (https://www.arsenaldining.cz) or give them a call at +420 222 311 090.

If you're in search of something a bit more refined but still deeply rooted in Czech culinary traditions, Café Imperial is the place to go. Located at Na Poříčí 15, 110 00 Praha 1, this iconic café serves both traditional Czech dishes and international fare, but what makes it special is its stunning art deco design and the way it brings an air of elegance to Czech dining. A favorite of mine is their goulash, which is always rich and flavorful, perfectly accompanied by freshly baked bread and a pint of Czech beer. Café Imperial is not just about the food—it's about experiencing the rich history of Prague as you dine. Prices here range from \$20 to \$40 for a main dish, and the atmosphere makes it worth every penny. For reservations, visit their website at (http://www.cafeimperial.cz) or call +420 221 111 111.

For those venturing out of Prague, Restaurace Na Farmářské in Plzeň, about 1.5 hours from the capital, is a must-visit for authentic Czech fare. Located at Smetanova 4, 301 00 Plzeň, this rustic restaurant serves dishes that showcase the flavors of the region, including a fantastic take on smažený sýr (fried cheese), pilsner-style sausages, and a variety of seasonal offerings. The ambiance is rustic and welcoming, with a focus on locally sourced ingredients. Meals here are reasonably priced, ranging from \$15 to \$30, and the portions are generous. If you find yourself in the area, it's definitely worth the trip. To learn more or to book a table, you can reach them at +420 377 053 270.

Lastly, no visit to the Czech Republic would be complete without trying some traditional koláče (Czech pastries), and for the best, I recommend stopping by Cukrárna Dobrý Časy, a local bakery in Brno. Located at Drobného 9, 602 00 Brno, this quaint pastry shop serves a variety of sweet and savory koláče, including options filled with poppy seeds, fruit, or even savory cheese. Prices for a koláč here are around $2 to $5, making it an affordable treat that's perfect for a mid-day snack. The shop has a cozy, welcoming vibe, and their pastries are freshly made, offering a true taste of Czech baking traditions. You can visit their website at (http://www.dobrycty.cz) or call +420 734 256 796 for more details.

When it comes to experiencing Czech cuisine, the country offers a range of dining spots that cater to every kind of food lover. Whether you're in the mood for a casual pub meal or a more refined dining experience, these restaurants give you an authentic taste of Czech culture.

Cafes and Bistros in Prague

When I think of the perfect way to spend a morning or afternoon in Prague, it's hard not to imagine myself sipping a perfectly brewed coffee in a charming café or indulging in a light meal at one of the city's cozy bistros. The café culture here is alive and well, and whether you're a dedicated coffee lover or someone who simply enjoys a relaxing atmosphere, the best cafes and bistros in Prague offer an unforgettable experience. Prague has a fantastic blend of old-world charm and modern style when it comes to dining spots, and in these spaces, you'll often find a perfect mix of the two.

One of my absolute favorites, and a must-visit for any coffee lover, is Café Louvre. Located at Národní 22, 110 00 Praha 1, this iconic café has been serving Prague since 1902, and it has a timeless appeal. When you walk in, you're immediately greeted by the stunning art nouveau décor and the feeling that you've stepped into history. Café Louvre is more than just a place for coffee—it's a spot where intellectuals, artists, and writers once gathered, and the vibe is still intellectual and relaxed. I personally love sitting by the window, watching the world go by while enjoying a rich espresso paired with a slice of traditional Czech apple strudel. The menu offers a variety of Czech and international options, with dishes like eggs Benedict and Czech-style open-faced sandwiches. The prices here are reasonable for the experience—expect to pay between $5 to $12 for a coffee and a pastry. You can easily get there by taking a tram to the Národní třída stop, just a short walk away from the café. Visit their website for more details: (https://www.cafelouvre.cz), or call them at +420 224 930 944.

Another gem in Prague is Café Savoy, which is a perfect blend of modern elegance and historical roots. Situated at Vítězná 124/5, 150 00 Praha 5, it feels like a Parisian café but with a distinct Prague twist. This café is housed in a beautifully restored space with high ceilings and grand windows that flood the room with light, creating an airy and inviting atmosphere. Whether you're looking to enjoy a rich coffee or indulge in a more substantial meal, Café Savoy has something to suit your needs. I've often spent hours here, sipping on their expertly crafted cappuccinos and savoring a traditional Czech breakfast or a savory quiche. The menu also includes French-style pastries and desserts, such as buttery croissants and decadent tarts. For a full meal, the prices range from $15 to $30 for a main course. It's easy to get to by tram or metro—just hop off at the Anděl metro station. Visit their website at (http://www.cafesavoy.cz) or call them at +420 257 530 072.

If you're in the mood for something a bit more modern and quirky, Můj šálek kávy in the Karlín district is an excellent choice. Located at Křižíkova 105, 186 00 Praha 8, this café is known for serving some of the best specialty coffee in Prague. The café has a minimalist design and a relaxed, no-fuss vibe that makes it a favorite for locals and tourists alike. Whether you're a black coffee enthusiast or you love a good flat white, the baristas here are experts and will recommend the perfect brew. I recommend trying their single-origin pour-over coffee, paired with a slice of homemade cake. Prices here are affordable, usually ranging from $3 to $8 for a coffee and a small snack. Getting there is easy—just take the metro to Křižíkova station, and you'll be right there. You can find more information on their website (https://www.mujsalekkavy.cz) or call them at +420 774 233 117.

For a more intimate bistro experience, Eska in the Karlin district is a modern take on traditional Czech cuisine. Located at Pernerova 49, 186 00 Praha 8, Eska combines rustic charm with modern innovation, offering both food and a great selection of natural wines. The interior is industrial and stylish, with open kitchens where you can watch the chefs prepare your meal. The menu is always changing, but you can expect to find fresh takes on classic Czech dishes, like their smoked meats and slow-cooked beef. I've had a fantastic experience here, particularly with their charred vegetables, and the bread they bake on-site is some of the best I've ever tasted. Prices are on the higher end, usually ranging from $20 to $35 for a full meal. You can easily reach Eska by taking the metro to Křižíkova or Florenc stations. Check out their website for more details: (https://www.eska.istanbul) or call them at +420 222 585 587.

Lastly, for a unique and cozy bistro experience, Bistro 8 located at Karlin 35, 186 00 Praha 8, offers simple but delicious food with a focus on seasonal ingredients. This place is tucked away in a quiet part of Prague, and it's perfect for a peaceful brunch or a light dinner. Whether you opt for their creamy soups, a flavorful salad, or one of their hearty sandwiches, you're sure to enjoy the food here. The atmosphere is laid-back and intimate, making it a great spot to relax with a book or have a casual meal with friends. The prices are quite reasonable, ranging from $10 to $18 for a main dish. To get there, take the metro to Křižíkova, and it's a short walk from there. Visit their website at (https://www.bistro8.cz) for more details or call +420 222 764 100.

Prague's cafés and bistros are a reflection of the city's charm and diversity—each one offering a unique experience, whether you're in the mood for a quick coffee or a leisurely meal. From traditional places that have been around for decades to trendy spots that keep things fresh, there's no shortage of options for those looking to explore the local café culture. Each time I visit, I find myself returning to these places, enjoying not just the food and drinks but also the atmosphere that makes each one so special.

Vegetarian and Vegan Options

When I first visited the Czech Republic, I wasn't sure what to expect in terms of vegetarian and vegan dining options. Given the country's rich meat-heavy culinary traditions, like svíčková (braised beef with creamy sauce) and knedlíky (dumplings often served with roast pork), I assumed finding plant-based meals would be a challenge. To my surprise, Prague has an exciting and growing scene for vegetarians and vegans, and I found that it wasn't difficult at all to find delicious, satisfying meals that fit my dietary preferences.

One of the first places that made me feel completely at home as a vegan was Maitrea, located in the heart of Prague at Týnská ulička 6, 110 00 Praha 1. This charming, cozy restaurant is one of the best vegetarian and vegan spots in the city. Its menu is entirely plant-based, offering an array of international flavors with a focus on fresh, organic ingredients. The tofu steak with miso sauce and the vegan lasagna were absolute favorites of mine. The atmosphere here is warm, with minimalist decor and a peaceful ambiance, making it the perfect spot for a relaxed meal after a day of sightseeing. Prices here are quite reasonable, with main dishes ranging from $10 to $18. You can reach Maitrea easily by taking a tram to Staroměstská station and walking just a few minutes. For more details, visit their website at (https://www.restauracemaitrea.cz) or call +420 222 221 500.

Another fantastic find was Vegan's Prague, located at Karoliny Světlé 12, 110 00 Praha 1. It's a vibrant, trendy spot where you can enjoy hearty, flavorful vegan dishes. Their vegan burgers and plant-based seitan skewers quickly became my go-to choices. The food here is bold and satisfying, catering not just to vegans but to anyone looking for a tasty and unique meal. What I loved most about Vegan's Prague was the great mix of both healthy options, like their superfood bowls, and indulgent comfort foods, such as their vegan goulash, which was a delicious twist on the classic Czech dish. Expect to spend about $12 to $20 for a full meal, and don't miss their homemade cakes for dessert. It's easy to reach by taking the metro to Staroměstská station and walking to the restaurant. Visit their website at (https://www.vegansprague.cz) or call them at +420 774 054 369.

If you're looking for a more casual café with a great variety of vegetarian and vegan options, Loving Hut (located at Sokolovská 101/42, 186 00 Praha 8) is a must-try. This global vegan chain has a spot in Prague, and it's one of those places where you can drop in for a quick, satisfying meal. The vegan pho was a standout dish for me—rich, flavorful, and perfect for a cold day. What's wonderful about Loving Hut is that it's not just about vegan food; it's about making plant-based meals accessible to everyone, with options that cater to all tastes. Prices are reasonable too, with meals typically ranging from $8 to $14. You can easily reach it by taking the metro to Křižíkova station. For more information, visit (https://www.lovinghut.cz) or call +420 222 315 245.

For those who enjoy a unique, fine-dining experience, Restaurant Eska in Karlin offers a refined yet plant-forward menu. Located at Pernerova 49, 186 00 Praha 8, Eska's approach to food is creative and fresh, with a focus on sustainability. The vegan fermented cabbage with dumplings was a surprising and delightful take on traditional Czech flavors. Eska also uses local, seasonal ingredients, so the menu changes regularly, offering something new each time. Expect to pay a little more here, with main dishes ranging from $20 to $35. It's a bit on the upscale side, but the innovative, thoughtful approach to plant-based dining makes it well worth the visit. To get there, take the metro to Křižíkova or Florenc stations. Visit their website at (https://www.eska.istanbul) or call +420 222 585 587.

Finally, for a spot that focuses on fresh, wholesome food in a more laid-back environment, Puro in the Vinohrady district is perfect. Located at Vinohradská 60, 130 00 Praha 3, this modern bistro offers a wide variety of vegetarian and vegan dishes, with options ranging from hearty salads to rich, flavorful stews. Their vegan risotto was one of the best I've had, packed with fresh vegetables and herbs. Puro prides itself on using local, organic ingredients, which really shows in the quality of the food. The atmosphere is welcoming and casual, making it a great choice for breakfast, brunch, or lunch. Prices are affordable, with dishes ranging from $10 to $18. You can get there by taking the metro to Jiřího z Poděbrad station. Visit their website at (http://www.puro.cz) or call +420 222 595 035.

Culinary Courses and Food Tours

When I visited the Czech Republic, one of the highlights of my trip was immersing myself in the country's rich culinary traditions. I've always believed that the best way to experience a culture is through its food, and the Czech Republic offers a unique opportunity to do just that. If you're a food lover like me, diving into the world of Czech cuisine through culinary courses and food tours is a fantastic way to not only learn more about the local dishes but also gain hands-on experience with authentic ingredients and recipes.

One of the first things I tried was a food tour in Prague. It was an unforgettable way to explore the city's vibrant food scene, and I highly recommend it for anyone visiting the Czech capital. I joined a Prague Food Tour, which offered a delightful 3-hour walking tour through the city's Old Town. The guide was incredibly knowledgeable, and I had the chance to taste a variety of traditional Czech foods, like trdelník (the sweet pastry often associated with Prague) and chlebíčky (Czech open-faced sandwiches). The tour also included a stop at a local beer hall where I learned about Czech beer culture—a must for anyone visiting the country. This food tour costs around $70 per person, which includes all food tastings, drinks, and the guide's expertise. It's easy to get to by public transport; I simply hopped on the metro and got off at Staroměstská station, which was just a short walk to the starting point. For more information, check out their website at (https://www.praguefoodtour.com).

Another great experience was with Czech Cooking Classes, located in the heart of Prague. If you've ever wanted to learn how to make a proper Czech meal from scratch, this is the place to go. During the class, I learned how to prepare traditional dishes like svíčková (braised beef with creamy sauce) and knedlíky (Czech dumplings), all under the guidance of an experienced local chef. It was a fun, interactive way to learn about the history and nuances of Czech cooking, and I left the class feeling more confident in my own cooking skills. The class lasted about four hours and cost approximately $90, which was a great value considering I left with recipes, cooking tips, and a full stomach! The cooking school is located at Vězeňská 9, 110 00 Praha 1, and it's easily accessible via the metro from Náměstí Republiky station. You can also visit their website at (http://www.czechcookingclasses.com) or call them at +420 775 740 089 to reserve your spot.

For those interested in a more specialized food tour, I recommend checking out Taste of Prague. This tour goes beyond the usual food tasting, diving into the city's evolving culinary scene, from traditional Czech meals to contemporary twists. We visited a combination of hidden gems—small local restaurants and food stalls that most tourists wouldn't find on their own. One of the standout moments was trying Smažený Sýr (fried cheese), a beloved Czech street food. The guide also took us to a few artisan food shops, where I learned about local Czech ingredients like svatojánský chléb (a type of Czech bread) and the famous Czech pickles. The tour is priced around $100, but it's well worth it if you want to experience Prague like a local. The meeting point for the tour is typically in the Old Town, just a short walk from Staroměstská metro station. You can book it on their website at (https://www.tasteofprague.com).

If you're traveling outside Prague, Czech Culinary Holidays in Southern Bohemia offers a lovely retreat. Located in České Budějovice, this program is perfect for anyone wanting a deeper dive into Czech cooking and lifestyle. The retreat includes a series of cooking workshops, where you'll learn to make dishes like bramboráky (potato pancakes) and kulajda (mushroom soup), all while staying in a charming countryside location. The program also includes guided tours of local markets, where you can pick fresh ingredients to use in the cooking classes. Prices for the program start at $250 for a two-day stay, which includes accommodation, meals, and all cooking classes. Getting there is simple by train from Prague, which takes around two and a half hours. More details can be found on their website at (http://www.czechculinaryholidays.com).

Whether you're a beginner cook or an experienced food enthusiast, these culinary experiences in the Czech Republic offer something for everyone. I found that food tours and cooking classes not only gave me a deeper appreciation for Czech cuisine but also a fun way to engage with locals and other travelers. The chance to try new ingredients, learn classic recipes, and experience the food culture firsthand really enhanced my trip. So, if you're planning to visit the Czech Republic, be sure to carve out some time for a food tour or cooking class—trust me, it'll be one of the most memorable parts of your journey!

CHAPTER 5

Shopping Insights

When I first set foot in the Czech Republic, one of the things I was most excited about was the chance to do some shopping. Not the kind of shopping you'd do in any major global city with all the big-name brands, but shopping for something truly local, unique, and rooted in tradition. I soon found out that the Czech Republic is a treasure trove of charming marketplaces, vibrant street vendors, and beautifully handcrafted souvenirs. Each item tells a story, and I couldn't wait to discover what made the shopping scene in this country so special.

Czech marketplaces, with their lively atmosphere and colorful stalls, are an absolute must-see. These open-air markets are where you'll find everything from fresh produce and local delicacies to intricate handicrafts and one-of-a-kind keepsakes. On my visit, I strolled through the bustling Havelské Tržiště in Prague, where I was surrounded by artisan goods, flowers, and handmade jewelry. The street vendors are just as delightful—whether it's a local selling homemade jams, a street artist offering a painting of Prague, or a craftsman offering wood carvings, the experience is a true celebration of Czech creativity.

If you're looking to take a piece of the country home with you, the Czech Republic has no shortage of traditional keepsakes. I found the perfect gift in the form of beautifully embroidered tablecloths and traditional Czech crystal glassware—items that reflect the country's long-standing artisan traditions. It was also fun to explore the regional specialties, like the famous Czech marionettes from the countryside or the colorful ceramics from the town of Český Krumlov. Every town and city in the country seems to have its own distinct take on craftsmanship, making each find even more meaningful.

In this chapter, I'll take you through some of the best shopping experiences in the Czech Republic, from vibrant marketplaces to the smaller, lesser-known shops that offer handcrafted treasures you can't find anywhere else. Whether you're looking for high-quality souvenirs to take home or simply want to explore the local culture through shopping, you'll find it here. Keep reading, and I'll share some of the best spots to pick up your own Czech keepsakes, and how to navigate the market scene like a local.

Marketplaces and Street Vendors

Exploring the Czech Republic's marketplaces and street vendors offers a vibrant window into the heart of its daily life and culture. During my travels, I made it a point to visit several markets across Prague and other cities, each offering a unique glimpse into the local lifestyle and an opportunity to engage directly with Czech traditions.

One of my favorite spots to visit was Havelské Tržiště in Prague. Located in the center of the city along Havelská street, between Mustek and Národní Třída metro stations, this marketplace is one of the oldest in Prague, dating back to 1232. The market is easily accessible by metro, with Mustek being the closest stop. As you wander through, you'll find stalls bursting with fresh fruits, vegetables, flowers, and souvenirs ranging from Czech marionettes to Bohemian crystal. It's a bustling atmosphere where locals shop for daily essentials and tourists discover unique keepsakes.

Each visit brings something new to the table, whether it's seasonal produce or handmade goods, making every stroll an adventure.

Another exceptional marketplace experience can be found at Naplavka Farmers Market. Located on the Rašínovo nábřeží embankment along the Vltava River, this Saturday market is a favorite among locals for its lively vibe and stunning river views. You can get there by tram, stopping at Palackého náměstí, or by metro at the Karlovo náměstí station. Here, local vendors sell everything from organic food to artisan breads and freshly brewed coffee. The market also serves as a social hotspot where people enjoy live music, savor street food, and sip beers under the Prague sky. It's not just a place to shop but a cultural gathering that highlights the communal spirit of the city.

In the charming town of Český Krumlov, the Český Krumlov Market on Široká Street is a smaller scale but equally enchanting option. This market brings the local community and tourists together in a picturesque setting. Vendors offer a variety of traditional Czech products, including hand-painted Easter eggs, wooden toys, and homemade preserves that are hard to find anywhere else. It's a short walk from any part of the small town and offers a lovely slice of regional culture and craftsmanship.

Visiting these markets isn't just about shopping; it's about experiencing the local lifestyle. The interaction with vendors, the taste of fresh, local produce, and the sight of traditional crafts create a rich tapestry of experiences that bring you closer to understanding the Czech way of life. Whether you're picking up ingredients for a meal, searching for the perfect souvenir, or just soaking up the lively atmosphere, the marketplaces and street vendors of the Czech Republic offer a unique cultural immersion that's as enriching as it is delightful.

Each market visit left me with not just souvenirs, but stories to tell and a deeper appreciation for the Czech people and their traditions. These markets are more than just places to buy goods—they are vibrant community centers where tradition meets everyday life. Whether you're a local or a traveler, spending time at these markets is an essential part of the Czech experience, providing insights into the country's culinary landscape, artistic expressions, and communal practices. So next time you find yourself in the Czech Republic, make sure to stroll through its markets, chat with the vendors, and let yourself be drawn into the heart of Czech culture.

Exclusive Shops in Prague's City Center

If you're looking to experience a more luxurious side of Prague, the city's exclusive shops in the heart of the city offer a shopping experience like no other. As someone who's spent hours wandering through the cobbled streets of Prague's center, I can tell you that these shops are more than just retail spaces—they're a testament to the city's blend of old-world charm and modern elegance. They provide an escape from the typical touristy routes and offer something unique for those with a taste for high-end fashion, art, and craftsmanship.

One of the first places you'll want to check out is Pařížská Street, located in the Old Town (Staré Město). This street is the Czech Republic's answer to Fifth Avenue or the Champs-Élysées, lined with some of the world's most famous luxury brands. You'll find the likes of Louis Vuitton, Prada, Gucci, and Chanel here, but what makes this street so special isn't just the high-end shops—it's the architecture. The facades of these stores are housed in historic buildings with intricate details, making for a picturesque shopping experience. To get there, simply head towards the Old Town Square, and Pařížská will be just a short walk away. It's easily accessible by tram or metro, with the Staroměstská stop being the closest.

During my stroll down Pařížská, I found myself popping into the smaller, boutique-style shops that pepper the street. These shops specialize in Czech-made luxury goods, from bespoke jewelry to handcrafted leather products. One standout is the Czech brand, BOHEMIA Crystal, a store offering the finest Bohemian glassware. The designs are exquisite, and the quality of the glass, some of which has been made using traditional methods passed down through generations, is unmatched. The store is located just off Pařížská Street, and I highly recommend taking the time to browse through its collection of crystal vases, glasses, and intricate decorative pieces. It's a great place to find a unique souvenir that captures the essence of Czech craftsmanship. You can also reach BOHEMIA Crystal via a short walk from the Old Town Square or take the metro to the Staroměstská stop.

If you're in the mood for high-end fashion but want to skip the global brands, you should head over to the boutique shops along Na Příkopě Street. This area is known for housing some of Prague's most refined Czech fashion labels. I visited a few of these stores, and each had something different to offer, whether it was bespoke suits from renowned local designers or beautiful leather handbags handmade in the Czech Republic. Stores like the elegant Sartoria L'Atelier, located at Na Příkopě 14, are a great place to find an impeccably tailored suit or luxurious accessories that you won't find elsewhere. The location is easily accessible by tram or metro, with the Můstck stop being just a few minutes away. But it's not all about clothing and accessories. Prague's exclusive shops also offer a taste of fine art and collectibles. One of the city's best-kept secrets is the Fine Art Gallery, located just off Wenceslas Square at Vodičkova 6. This gallery features works by local artists as well as classic pieces that showcase the evolution of Czech art. I visited this gallery on a rainy afternoon, and the calm atmosphere allowed me to truly appreciate the beauty of Czech art. It's a perfect stop for anyone looking to take home a piece of authentic Czech culture. You can easily get there by walking from Wenceslas Square or hopping on the metro and getting off at the Muzeum stop.

Lastly, no trip to Prague's luxury shopping scene is complete without stopping by the "Vinohradská" district. While it is not typically associated with exclusive luxury brands, Vinohrady is home to several upscale antique shops and high-end local design studios. Walking around this neighborhood, I found a stunning shop dedicated to fine Czech porcelain, offering hand-painted pieces that felt like true works of art. It's a short tram ride from the city center, and I would recommend getting off at the Náměstí Míru station for easy access to some of the best antiques and collectible art pieces the city has to offer.

Whether you're after a luxury handbag, hand-blown glass, or a piece of Czech artwork, Prague's exclusive shops offer something for everyone with an eye for quality and design. For me, shopping in this city was never just about purchasing an item—it was about immersing myself in the stories behind the products. Each shop and boutique is a reflection of the country's rich heritage and a celebration of local craftsmanship, making them well worth a visit for anyone looking to take a piece of Prague's unique elegance home.

Keepsakes: Traditional Czech Products, Regional Souvenirs and Handicrafts

When I first arrived in the Czech Republic, I was immediately struck by how rich the country's cultural heritage is, especially when it comes to the traditional products and regional handicrafts that fill the streets, shops, and markets. There's something incredibly special about taking home a piece of a country's soul, and Czech keepsakes do just that. From intricate glassware to hand-painted pottery, the craft traditions here are centuries old, and the local artisans are fiercely proud of their heritage. So, if you're looking for a souvenir that's as much about the experience as it is about the item itself, these traditional Czech products will not disappoint.

One of the most iconic Czech products you'll find is Bohemian glass, which has been crafted in this region for hundreds of years. I remember walking through the Old Town of Prague and stumbling upon a small crystal shop tucked between two grand buildings. The sparkling display of hand-blown glass vases, bowls, and intricate chandeliers caught my eye immediately. The craftsmanship is extraordinary, with each piece reflecting the meticulous care and skill that goes into making these pieces. You'll find many shops in Prague that specialize in this beautiful glassware, but I recommend visiting places like Bohemia Crystal at Pařížská Street, where the glass is crafted using techniques passed down for generations. These pieces often have a modern twist while still honoring traditional methods, making them a perfect gift or keepsake. Expect to pay anywhere from $30 to $300, depending on the complexity and size of the item.

Another traditional Czech product that you can't miss is the famous Czech porcelain. This delicate porcelain has been a hallmark of Czech craftsmanship for centuries. I had the pleasure of visiting a small, charming shop called Český Porcelán, located in the city center. There, I found delicate tea sets, hand-painted plates, and charming figurines, each with vibrant designs that are steeped in tradition. The porcelain here is known for its fine quality and beauty, and I was particularly taken by the hand-painted designs that often feature traditional Czech motifs, such as flowers, birds, and folklore scenes. These pieces make wonderful gifts or souvenirs for anyone who appreciates fine craftsmanship. Prices can range from $20 for a small piece like a plate to $150 or more for a complete set.

But perhaps the most unexpected and delightful souvenirs I came across were the traditional Czech wooden toys. I had heard about them before my trip, but seeing them in person was something else entirely. These handcrafted toys are made using techniques that have been passed down through generations, and they are a true reflection of Czech folk traditions. I stumbled upon a lovely store called Dřevěné Hračky, which specializes in wooden toys. The toys range from simple spinning tops to beautifully crafted dolls and puzzles, and I found them to be incredibly charming. They are often brightly painted in vivid colors, with designs that range from classic to whimsical. Prices for these handcrafted toys are relatively affordable, with items ranging from $10 to $40, depending on size and complexity. They're perfect for children or anyone wanting a piece of the Czech folk culture to take home.

Of course, when you think of Czech souvenirs, you can't overlook the traditional Czech beer mugs and steins, which are as much a part of Czech history as the beer itself. Czech beer culture is legendary, and the beer mugs are just as iconic. I picked up a beautifully decorated ceramic beer mug in a shop near the Old Town Square, and it's now one of my favorite keepsakes. These mugs are often handmade, and many feature elaborate engravings or hand-painted designs depicting local landmarks, historical figures, or Czech folklore. The prices for these beer mugs typically range from \$20 to \$50, and you'll find them in most souvenir shops, especially those catering to tourists in Prague.

Then there's the world of Czech folk art, where you can find a huge variety of hand-painted wooden items, lacework, and embroidered textiles. If you want to take home something truly unique, Czech folk art is an excellent choice. One of my favorite discoveries was a shop called Czech Folk Art, located near Wenceslas Square, where I found intricate lacework and beautifully embroidered tablecloths and scarves. These items are often hand-stitched, and they carry with them the charm of the Czech countryside, where such skills are still passed down through generations. The prices for these items vary, but you can expect to pay anywhere from \$15 for a small embroidered handkerchief to \$100 for a larger tablecloth or scarf.

As I explored more of the Czech countryside, I discovered that each region has its own specialty when it comes to handicrafts. For example, in Moravia, you'll find beautiful hand-woven textiles, often used in the region's folk costumes, while in the southern Czech region, you can pick up traditional wooden toys that are made by hand in small villages. I was fortunate enough to visit some of these areas during my travels, and I loved discovering the different regional crafts that are as diverse as the landscape itself.

Getting your hands on these unique products isn't difficult. Prague's Old Town is a treasure trove of shops offering these items, but you can also find them at local markets, particularly around Christmas time when the markets are filled with local artisans displaying their handmade goods. The Prague Christmas Market at the Old Town Square is one of the best places to find these traditional Czech keepsakes. Alternatively, many of these products can be found in specialty shops and boutiques throughout the city, or if you venture a little outside the city, you can explore markets in smaller towns for an even more authentic experience.

Whether you're in the city or the countryside, you'll find that the traditional Czech products and regional handicrafts available are more than just souvenirs—they're a reflection of the country's history, culture, and the artistry that continues to thrive here. When I look at the items I brought back, each one reminds me of the craftsmanship and dedication of the people who made them, and I can't help but feel like I've brought a piece of Czech history home with me.

CHAPTER 6

Attractions and Activities

When I first arrived in the Czech Republic, I was immediately struck by how much this country has to offer for a curious traveler. It's a place where history, culture, and natural beauty converge, providing visitors with a vast array of attractions and activities to explore. Whether you're wandering through the cobbled streets of Prague, hiking in the Krkonoše Mountains, or discovering the artistic pulse of Brno and Olomouc, the Czech Republic invites you to immerse yourself in its rich past and vibrant present.

In the capital, Prague, I found myself captivated by the timeless beauty of Prague Castle, an imposing structure that tells the story of centuries of Czech history. The nearby Charles Bridge, with its statues and sweeping views of the Vltava River, felt like a journey back in time. Then, there's the Old Town Square, where the Astronomical Clock comes to life every hour, drawing crowds of awe-struck visitors like myself. It's easy to get lost in Prague's charm, but beyond the city's famous landmarks, there's so much more to explore, from the thought-provoking National Museum to the intriguing Museum of Communism, where I learned about the country's more recent past.

If you're a nature lover or an adventure seeker, you'll find plenty to keep you busy too. I had a blast trying river rafting along the Vltava and spent an unforgettable weekend hiking in the Krkonoše Mountains, the highest range in the Czech Republic. If you're into outdoor activities, these mountains are a playground, with trails for every level of hiker and breathtaking views to match. For something a little different, a day trip to Karlštejn Castle or the UNESCO-listed town of Kutná Hora can easily be worked into your itinerary. These destinations are perfect examples of how the Czech Republic blends its medieval past with modern-day exploration.

Outside of Prague, I had the chance to discover Brno, a city with a youthful energy and a mix of contemporary culture and history, and Olomouc, which stole my heart with its artistic vibe and beautiful Baroque architecture. Both cities are far less touristy than Prague, but that's what makes them so special—they offer an authentic slice of Czech life that I don't think I'll ever forget.

In this chapter, I'll take you on a journey through all of these attractions and activities, highlighting the must-see sites and the hidden gems that will make your visit to the Czech Republic unforgettable. Whether you're a history buff, an art lover, an adventurer, or someone simply looking to soak in the beauty of this country, you'll find something here that will capture your imagination and leave you with lasting memories.

Prague's Cultural Heritage

When I first set foot in Prague, I was immediately swept away by the city's rich cultural heritage. The kind of place where every street, building, and square tells a story. It's not just the famous landmarks that make this city so special, but the deep history that lies beneath the surface, waiting to be discovered by anyone willing to take the time to look. I've been fortunate enough to experience Prague's cultural tapestry firsthand, and it's truly a city that wears its history with pride, offering an unforgettable journey through time.

Prague's historical significance can't be overstated. The city has been at the crossroads of European culture, politics, and history for centuries. From the medieval period to its pivotal role during the Austro-Hungarian Empire, and its later transformation through communism and the Velvet Revolution, Prague's cultural heritage is shaped by the events that unfolded within its walls. Every building, from the Gothic spires of St. Vitus Cathedral to the elegant Baroque architecture of the Old Town, seems to whisper tales of the past.

One of the most striking aspects of Prague's cultural heritage is how it blends architectural styles from different periods. The Old Town, with its cobblestone streets and medieval buildings, feels like stepping into a fairytale. I spent hours just wandering around the Old Town Square, soaking in the beauty of the Astronomical Clock, which dates back to the 15th century. As it struck the hour, tourists gathered around, eagerly waiting for the mechanical show that's been mesmerizing visitors for centuries. Just behind the square, the narrow streets are lined with charming cafés, galleries, and shops, each with its own story to tell.

Then there's Prague Castle, perched high above the city, a majestic reminder of the country's royal past. Walking through the castle's halls, I was transported to a time when kings and queens ruled the land, and the castle served as the political heart of the Czech Kingdom. The Golden Lane, with its tiny houses, almost seemed frozen in time, offering a glimpse into what life was like for those who lived and worked within the castle walls.

But Prague's cultural heritage isn't just confined to its stunning architecture. The city is home to a thriving arts scene, with museums and galleries showcasing everything from ancient artifacts to contemporary works. The National Museum is a must-see, housing vast collections that chronicle the country's natural history, while the Mucha Museum is dedicated to the art of Alphonse Mucha, one of the Czech Republic's most famous artists. His iconic Art Nouveau works can be found across Prague, adding a touch of elegance and grace to the city's artistic landscape.

What truly struck me about Prague was how its cultural heritage is so deeply embedded in everyday life. Whether it's the traditional Czech music playing in a café, the artists painting in the public squares, or the food markets offering local delicacies, Prague is a city that celebrates its history at every turn. Even a simple walk through the city feels like you're experiencing a living museum. I spent a delightful afternoon at the Náplavka Farmers' Market, which runs along the Vltava River, where I sampled fresh Czech pastries and chatted with locals, all while taking in the views of the city's historic skyline.

The city is also home to a fascinating mix of historical sites that explore its more recent past. The Museum of Communism, for instance, is a powerful reminder of the country's experience under Soviet rule, providing insight into the challenges and triumphs of the Czech people during this time. For a more in-depth look at Prague's layered history, a visit to the Jewish

Quarter is a must. Here, you can explore the Jewish Museum and visit the poignant Old Jewish Cemetery, one of the oldest of its kind in Europe.

Throughout my time in Prague, I came to realize that the city's cultural heritage is not something locked away in museums or historical sites; it's something that lives and breathes in the heart of the city. It's in the rhythm of daily life, in the conversations between strangers, and in the warmth of a Czech welcome. Prague isn't just a place to visit—it's a place to experience, to step into a living piece of history that's both timeless and ever-changing. For anyone visiting Prague, diving into its cultural heritage is one of the most rewarding parts of the journey. Whether you're marveling at its architecture, immersing yourself in its artistic offerings, or simply walking through its historic streets, you'll be constantly reminded that you're standing in the midst of a city with a story to tell, a city that invites you to become a part of its ongoing narrative.

Notable Sites: Prague Castle, Charles Bridge, Old Town Square and the Astronomical Clock

During my time in Prague, I made sure to explore the iconic sites that truly define the city's character: Prague Castle, Charles Bridge, Old Town Square, and the Astronomical Clock. These landmarks are not just tourist destinations, but symbols of Prague's deep history, blending architecture, culture, and storytelling in a way that's both captivating and educational.

Let's start with Prague Castle, which, at over 1,000 years old, is a must-see for anyone visiting the city. Perched high above the city, it's not only the largest ancient castle in the world but also a symbol of the Czech state. I made my way up the hill from the Lesser Town, and as I approached the castle complex, I could feel the history pressing in from all sides. The castle itself is a mix of Gothic, Romanesque, and Baroque architecture, with its most notable feature being

St. Vitus Cathedral, whose soaring spires dominate the skyline. I recommend spending at least half a day here, as there's so much to see: the Old Royal Palace, the colorful Golden Lane, and the tranquil gardens offer a real insight into the royal history of Prague. You can walk around freely in the castle grounds, but to get into the various buildings, like the cathedral or the Old Royal Palace, there's an entrance fee, which ranges from about $10 to $15 (250-350 CZK), depending on what areas you want to visit. The Castle is open daily from 9:00 AM to 5:00 PM, and you can easily get there by tram (No. 22, getting off at Pražský hrad).

Next up is the Charles Bridge, which I found to be one of the most picturesque and photogenic places in the city. The bridge, which spans the Vltava River, was completed in the 15th century and connects the Old Town with the Lesser Town. Walking across the bridge is a bit like stepping into history; you're surrounded by 30 statues of saints that line both sides, each offering their own story and significance. What's especially lovely is that, while it's always busy, the atmosphere never feels rushed. It's a place where you can pause, take in the views of the river and the Prague Castle looming in the background, and watch street performers. The best time to visit is early in the morning when it's less crowded, and you can really take in the tranquility of the bridge. There's no fee to cross, and it's easily accessible by foot from either side of the city—just follow the Vltava River, and you won't miss it.

Old Town Square is another landmark that I found to be full of life and energy. This historic square, located in the heart of Prague's Old Town, is one of the oldest and most beautiful public spaces in the city. It's surrounded by colorful buildings that range from Gothic to Baroque in style, each one more charming than the last. One of the first things I did when I arrived was find a seat at one of the outdoor cafes and simply watch the world go by. But Old Town Square is not just about the view—it's also home to Prague's famous Astronomical Clock, one of the oldest and most intricate clocks in the world. At the top of every hour, a crowd gathers to watch the clock's mechanical show, where the figures of the Twelve Apostles rotate, and the skeleton (representing Death) rings the bell. It's one of those little rituals that makes Prague feel so special. The square is free to wander around, and if you're feeling adventurous, climb the Old Town Hall tower for an incredible panoramic view of the city—tickets for this are about $8-$10 (200-250 CZK).

Each of these sites—Prague Castle, Charles Bridge, Old Town Square, and the Astronomical Clock—offers something different but equally memorable. They give you a glimpse into Prague's rich history and its blend of different architectural styles, from medieval to Baroque.

Museums: National Museum, Mucha Museum, Museum of Communism

When I first arrived in Prague, one of the first things I did was explore the city's incredible museums, each offering a different but equally rich perspective on Czech culture and history. Three museums in particular stood out to me—each providing an essential part of the cultural puzzle that is Prague: the National Museum, the Mucha Museum, and the Museum of Communism. These places are not just typical tourist attractions; they are windows into the soul of the Czech Republic, showcasing everything from its ancient past to its turbulent 20th-century history.

Let's start with the National Museum, a must-visit for anyone interested in the country's history. Located at the top of Wenceslas Square, this grand neoclassical building is hard to miss. As soon as I walked through the doors, I was immersed in a world of history that spans millions of years. The

National Museum covers everything from prehistoric fossils to medieval artifacts, but it's the collection that covers the history of Czechoslovakia that really caught my attention.

The museum gives a detailed overview of the country's rise and fall throughout the 20th century, especially the turbulent years under communist rule and the eventual transition to democracy. The exhibits are thoughtfully curated, making complex historical events feel accessible to anyone, regardless of their background. It was fascinating to see artifacts from the World War II era, including old military uniforms and letters. But my favorite part was learning about the Velvet Revolution and seeing how the Czechs peacefully fought for their freedom. A visit to the National Museum is an immersive experience that not only educates but also reminds you of the resilience of the Czech people. If you're an art lover, the Mucha Museum should be on your list. Located near the Old Town, the Mucha Museum is dedicated to the life and works of Alphonse Mucha, one of the most celebrated artists of the Art Nouveau movement. The museum is housed in a beautiful, intimate space and provides a deep dive into Mucha's most famous works, including his iconic posters of Sarah Bernhardt. I loved how the museum didn't just showcase his art but also gave a glimpse into his life and his deep connection to his Czech heritage.

Mucha's posters, with their flowing lines, delicate colors, and ethereal figures, are not just beautiful—they're full of meaning, often conveying messages of Czech national pride. The museum offers a fascinating look at how Mucha's work was tied to the cultural and political movements of his time. One of the highlights for me was seeing some of his lesser-known works, including his grand series of paintings based on Czech history and mythology. The Mucha Museum is a place that art lovers and history buffs alike will appreciate for its thoughtful and engaging displays. The Museum of Communism, on the other hand, was an entirely different but equally compelling experience. This museum offers a poignant look into life under the Communist regime, focusing on the years between 1948 and 1989. It's located just off Wenceslas Square, so it's easy to find.

What struck me most was the way the museum brought the past to life. It didn't just focus on political theory—it told the personal stories of the people who lived through this period. There were plenty of photographs, news clippings, and objects that told the story of how life in Prague was shaped by censorship, surveillance, and propaganda. The museum also highlighted the way ordinary people fought back, culminating in the Velvet Revolution, which led to the end of Communist rule. The museum does an excellent job of showing both the oppression of the regime and the strength of the Czech people in resisting it. It was a stark reminder of how recent the country's transition to democracy is and how much it has achieved since then.

Each of these museums left me with a deeper understanding of the Czech Republic, not just as a place but as a people. They provide unique windows into the Czech experience—whether through art, history, or the story of political struggle.

River Rafting and Outdoor Adventures

During my time in the Czech Republic, I had the opportunity to dive into some of the most exciting outdoor adventures, and one of the most thrilling activities I experienced was river rafting. For those who enjoy a good splash of adrenaline, river rafting is a fantastic way to explore the Czech landscape from a completely different perspective. Whether you're paddling down the Vltava River in Prague or navigating through the wild waters of the country's mountain regions, the Czech Republic offers a diverse range of river rafting experiences suited for beginners and seasoned adventurers alike.

Heading into the mountains, the Czech Republic offers a variety of ski resorts that are perfect for winter sports enthusiasts. The Špindlerův Mlýn Ski Resort stands out as a prime destination. Located in the heart of the Krkonoše Mountains, it provides a range of slopes suitable for all skill levels. The resort features modern facilities and stunning mountain views, making it a popular choice for both skiing and snowboarding. The resort is accessible by bus from Prague, which takes about two hours and drops you directly in the resort area.

One of the most popular rafting routes in Prague is along the Vltava River. It offers a scenic journey through the city's most iconic landmarks. As I made my way down the river, I was struck by how peaceful it felt to be in the heart of the city while still surrounded by nature. The river flows right past Prague Castle and Charles Bridge, and the view from the water is unlike anything I had seen from the streets. This rafting trip is more about sightseeing than thrill-seeking, so it's great for families or those looking for a more relaxed adventure. You can rent rafts or kayaks from companies like Rafting Prague (located near the city center), and the cost typically ranges from $20 to $40 per person for a half-day experience. Getting to the rental points is easy by public transportation. Most companies are located near the Czech National Theatre (Národní divadlo), which is a short walk from the nearest metro station, Staroměstská on Line A.

For those seeking a bit more excitement, I highly recommend heading out of the city to explore the Krkonošsko mountains, located in the northeastern part of the country. The Krkonošsko region, known for its rugged terrain and wild rivers, offers some of the best white-water rafting experiences in the country. I joined a rafting tour along the Labe River (also known as the Elbe River), which offers rapids suitable for those who enjoy the thrill of navigating through choppy waters. The river's mix of tranquil stretches and sudden rapids gives you the chance to both relax and challenge your paddling skills. The Elbe also flows through some beautiful natural scenery, making the rafting experience feel both adventurous and peaceful at the same time. To get to Krkonošsko, I took a train from Prague's main station to Liberec, which took about two hours. From there, local transport can take you to the rafting base where tours are organized. Expect to pay around $40 to $80 per person for a full-day rafting tour.

If you're looking to go rafting in a completely different environment, consider the Morava River near Olomouc, a picturesque city known for its historic charm. While this river is less intense than the Elbe, it still offers fun rapids and an opportunity to explore the beautiful countryside. I found this area to be less crowded, which made for a peaceful experience on the water. Rafting on the Morava River is typically arranged by local adventure companies, and the price varies depending on the length of the trip, but it's usually in the range of $30 to $60 per person. Getting to Olomouc is straightforward, as it's just a 2.5-hour train ride from Prague. Aside from river rafting, the Czech Republic offers a range of other outdoor activities that I found equally thrilling.

Hiking and cycling are extremely popular, especially in areas like Bohemian Switzerland National Park. The park is home to incredible rock formations, deep valleys, and dense forests. I spent an entire day hiking through the park's trails, and I was amazed by how pristine and untouched the area felt. It was the perfect escape from the hustle and bustle of Prague. If hiking is more your speed, the Krkonošsko Mountains offer a number of excellent trails, many of which lead to awe-inspiring views of the countryside.

The Šumava National Park, located along the Czech-Austrian border, is another outdoor paradise. Here, I found a variety of activities, including mountain biking and cross-country skiing in the winter months. The trails wind through lush forests and lead to serene lakes, giving you the chance to connect with nature in a way that's rare to find in most other parts of Europe. For anyone interested in combining nature with adventure, I highly recommend heading to the Czech Paradise (Český ráj) region, known for its beautiful sandstone rock formations. There, you can hike, rock climb, or simply explore the forested trails that meander through the rocky landscape.

Getting to many of these outdoor adventure spots is easy. The Czech Republic has an excellent public transportation system, including trains, buses, and even trams that make it simple to travel between cities and into more remote areas. Once you arrive in these regions, local companies often provide the necessary equipment and guided tours to ensure you have a safe and enjoyable experience. In terms of overall pricing for these outdoor activities, most rafting trips start at around $20 for a basic half-day tour, with more adventurous options, like those in the Krkonošsko mountains or Morava River, ranging from $40 to $80 per person for a full-day experience. It's also possible to rent gear for mountain biking or hiking at various outdoor centers, with prices typically starting at $10 to $20 per day. If you're thinking of booking a multi-day adventure, look for packages that include transport, equipment, and accommodations.

Adventures in the Krkonoše Mountains

The Krkonoše Mountains, also known as the Giant Mountains, are one of the Czech Republic's most stunning natural treasures, and I found them to be the perfect destination for an unforgettable outdoor adventure. Located in the northeastern part of the country, the Krkonoše range is the highest in the Czech Republic, with its highest peak, Sněžka, towering at 1,603 meters (5,259 feet). The mountains are part of a protected national park, Krkonošsko, which spans both the Czech Republic and Poland, offering a pristine landscape of dense forests, alpine meadows, cascading waterfalls, and, of course, breathtaking panoramic views.

The first time I visited the Krkonoše Mountains, I was struck by the contrast to Prague's urban sprawl. It felt like stepping into a completely different world, where nature's beauty was on full display at every turn. Getting to Krkonošsko is quite easy from Prague, as there are regular train and bus connections to the main town of Liberec, which is about a two-hour journey by train. From there, it's a short bus or taxi ride to several popular mountain towns like Harrachov, Špindlerův Mlýn, and Liberec, all of which serve as gateways to the Krkonoše National Park. If you're in Prague, you can catch a direct train to Liberec from the main railway station, Hlavní nádraží, or take a bus from Florenc Bus Station.

The Krkonoše Mountains offer a range of outdoor activities throughout the year, but I found the best time to visit was during the warmer months when hiking trails come alive. One of the most popular routes is the hike up to Sněžka, the tallest peak in the range. The hike is not for the faint of heart, but the views from the top are absolutely worth the effort. The trail is well-marked, and there are several routes to choose from, each offering different levels of difficulty. I chose a medium-level path from the town of Pec pod Sněžkou, which took about four hours to ascend.

Along the way, I passed through alpine meadows, thick forests, and crystal-clear streams, which made the journey feel both peaceful and invigorating. At the summit of Sněžka, I was met with a 360-degree view of the surrounding mountains and, on a clear day, the distant Polish countryside. There's also a small chapel and a weather station at the top, as well as a cable car station for those who prefer not to hike.

The cable car ride down is a fantastic way to take in the mountain landscape from a different perspective. If you're more inclined to take it easy, there are plenty of scenic spots throughout the Krkonošsko region that don't require climbing to the summit, such as the routes around Špindlerův Mlýn. The town itself is a popular base for hikers and skiers alike, and from there, you can find a number of scenic trails, including the beautifully picturesque Labská bouda, a mountain hut by the Elbe River. For those seeking a bit more thrill, the Krkonoše Mountains are a paradise for winter sports enthusiasts. When I visited during the ski season, I took full advantage of the ski resorts in Špindlerův Mlýn and Harrachov, which are the two largest ski areas in the country. Both offer excellent skiing and snowboarding options, with well-groomed slopes for all levels. I was particularly impressed by Harrachov's ski jumps, which are among the most famous in the country, attracting top-level athletes. Even if you're not a skier, there are plenty of other activities to enjoy during the winter months, including snowshoeing, tobogganing, and ice climbing.

But even outside of the summer and winter seasons, the Krkonoše Mountains have something to offer. In the spring and autumn, when the weather is milder, the mountains transform into a quiet haven for nature lovers. I spent a peaceful afternoon in the autumn, hiking through the golden forests and spotting wild animals such as deer and foxes. The fall colors were absolutely mesmerizing, with the trees turning brilliant shades of orange, yellow, and red. While hiking and skiing are the most popular activities, the Krkonoše region also offers excellent mountain biking trails, which I found to be an exhilarating way to explore the landscape. There are several bike rental shops in towns like Špindlerův Mlýn, and the trails range from easy, family-friendly paths to more challenging downhill runs for adrenaline junkies. If you're looking for something a bit more relaxing, the region is also home to several spas and wellness resorts, offering the perfect opportunity to unwind after a day of outdoor adventure.

For those interested in the flora and fauna of the region, Krkonošsko National Park is a designated biosphere reserve, which means it's home to a wide variety of unique species. I had the chance to visit the Krkonoš National Park Visitor Centre, located in the town of Liberec, which offers insightful exhibits about the local wildlife and the region's environmental protection efforts. The park is a UNESCO biosphere reserve, so the biodiversity here is truly remarkable. The best way to explore the Krkonoše Mountains is to stay in one of the charming mountain resorts, which are scattered throughout the region. Many of these offer a range of accommodations, from basic mountain cabins to luxury hotels with all the amenities. I stayed in Špindlerův Mlýn, where I was able to easily access the hiking trails, ski slopes, and even enjoy a traditional Czech meal at one of the local restaurants. Most of the accommodations offer shuttle services to the nearby trailheads, so getting around is fairly easy once you're settled in.

For anyone visiting the Krkonoše Mountains, I highly recommend packing good hiking shoes, plenty of water, and layers of clothing as the weather can change rapidly, even in the summer. And don't forget your camera – the scenery here is absolutely stunning and well worth capturing.

Brno: The Vibrant City Life

Brno, the second-largest city in the Czech Republic, has a vibrancy that's uniquely its own. While Prague may dominate the country's tourist scene, Brno is often overlooked, and that's a real shame. I had the pleasure of spending a few days there, and what struck me immediately was how effortlessly the city blends its rich history with modern energy, creating a cultural landscape that's as dynamic as it is welcoming.

Situated in the southeastern part of the country, Brno is the capital of the South Moravian region. It's a hub of student life, thanks to its top universities, and the atmosphere feels youthful and fresh. But that doesn't mean it's all just about academics. Brno has a surprising number of historical landmarks, cutting-edge design, lively nightlife, and a laid-back charm that makes it the perfect destination for those looking to experience a more local side of Czech life. Getting to Brno is easy, and I found the city very accessible whether you're arriving by train, bus, or car. If you're coming from Prague, it's just about a two-and-a-half-hour train ride on the fast InterCity line from Hlavní nádraží (the main train station), or you can take a bus from the Florenc bus station. Brno is also well-connected by road, and if you're driving from Prague, the journey takes about 2 hours and 15 minutes. The city's central location makes it a great base for exploring the surrounding wine regions and charming small towns of South Moravia.

As I explored Brno, I quickly realized how much the city had to offer. The historical center is compact and walkable, perfect for wandering without a strict itinerary. The iconic Špilberk Castle, sitting on a hill above the city, provides both a rich glimpse into the past and sweeping views of Brno's vibrant urban landscape. The castle's history is fascinating—it once served as a royal residence, a military fortress, and even a notorious prison. I spent a few hours wandering its museum, which showcases everything from medieval artifacts to 20th-century military history. The views from the castle are spectacular, so be sure to have your camera ready. A short walk from Špilberk leads you to the Cathedral of St. Peter and Paul, another of Brno's must-see landmarks. The towering spires of the cathedral dominate the city skyline, and inside, the intricate Gothic architecture is simply stunning. For history lovers, I highly recommend taking a tour to fully appreciate the cathedral's significance, including its connection to the 19th-century battles that shaped the region.

But Brno isn't just about history. The city's contemporary side is just as compelling. The Modernist-style Villa Tugendhat, a UNESCO World Heritage site, was a highlight for me. This stunning building, designed by the famous architect Ludwig Mies van der Rohe, is considered a masterpiece of modern architecture. It offers a rare glimpse into the elegant, minimalist design of the early 20th century, and the guided tour is fascinating, giving insight into both the design process and the tumultuous history of the villa. Brno's culture also comes alive in its cafes, restaurants, and nightlife. I was especially taken with the café culture, which is a key part of the city's social life. One of the standout spots I visited was Café Podnebí, a cozy little café tucked away in the city center. With its inviting atmosphere and excellent coffee, it felt like the perfect place to sit and people-watch.

If you're after something a little more modern, check out the Super Panda Circus, a stylish bar known for its innovative cocktails and vibrant décor. Whether you're in the mood for an afternoon coffee, an evening drink, or a late-night club experience, Brno has something for everyone. For food lovers, Brno has an impressive range of dining options. I dined at several fantastic places during my time there, but the one that stood out the most was Restaurace 4Pokoje.

This hidden gem offers a fusion of Czech and international flavors in a beautifully designed space. The menu is inventive yet comforting, and the service is top-notch. For a more traditional Czech meal, you can't go wrong with the classic pub food at U Dvou Kohoutů, a local favorite for hearty meals and a great selection of Czech beers.

If you're looking to stay in Brno, there are plenty of options to choose from, ranging from stylish hotels to cozy guesthouses. I stayed at the Hotel Barcelo Brno Palace, located just a short walk from the city center. This upscale hotel offers modern amenities, including a wellness center, fitness facilities, and an excellent restaurant. The rooms are spacious and comfortable, and the service was exceptional. Rates typically range from $100 to $150 per night, depending on the season and availability. Another great option is the City Hotel, located near the Brno Exhibition Centre. This is a more budget-friendly choice, with rooms averaging between $60 and $100 per night. It's perfect for those who want to be close to the city's main events and business areas, as well as offering easy access to public transport. When it comes to getting around Brno, I found the public transportation system to be highly efficient. The city's tram and bus network is extensive and easy to navigate, with tickets available for purchase at machines or via mobile apps. For a more relaxed experience, you can rent a bike or use the city's bike-sharing service to explore at your own pace. If you're planning to travel further, the city is well-served by regional train and bus services, making it easy to take day trips to nearby places like the famous wine region of Mikulov or the historic town of Kroměříž.

Olomouc: The Artistic Haven

Olomouc, nestled in the heart of Moravia, is a city that quietly pulses with creativity and history. Often overshadowed by Prague and Brno, Olomouc is a hidden gem that draws you in with its rich art scene, charming atmosphere, and fascinating blend of old-world beauty and modern energy. My time there was like stepping into a living canvas, a place where every corner seems to have a story to tell. Whether you're an art enthusiast or just someone who enjoys discovering places with character, Olomouc offers a rare opportunity to experience a city that feels both timeless and refreshingly vibrant.

Situated about two hours east of Brno by train, Olomouc is an easily accessible city. The journey from Brno is comfortable and scenic, passing through lush landscapes that give you a taste of the Moravian countryside. Upon arrival, I found the city's compact center to be effortlessly walkable, making it ideal for exploring on foot.

The main train station, which is well-connected to cities across the Czech Republic, is just a short tram or bus ride from the city center, so getting around is simple. For those driving, Olomouc is well-connected by highways, and there's plenty of parking available near the city center.

What struck me first about Olomouc was its remarkable balance of artistic expression and historical depth. The city is home to some of the most important Baroque architecture in the country, with stunning buildings like the Holy Trinity Column— a UNESCO World Heritage site that stands proudly in the center of the city. Its ornate carvings and sculptures depict religious scenes and figures, and the column itself is an iconic symbol of Olomouc's history and artistic culture. Beyond the architectural landmarks, Olomouc is a haven for anyone interested in the arts. The city is known for its vibrant cultural life, with numerous galleries, theaters, and art spaces. The Olomouc Museum of Art (OMU) was a highlight of my visit. Located in a former Franciscan monastery, the museum houses an impressive collection of Czech modern art, including works from the 20th and 21st centuries. As someone who appreciates art, I was captivated by the museum's ability to showcase both emerging artists and the greats of the past. The space itself is thoughtfully curated, with an intimate atmosphere that allows you to immerse yourself in the art.

Nearby, the St. Wenceslas Cathedral is another must-see. As you approach this magnificent Gothic church, you can't help but be struck by its sheer scale and beauty. Inside, the stained glass windows tell stories from the Bible, casting colorful light across the stone floors. The cathedral is also home to a crypt and an impressive bell tower, where you can climb to the top for panoramic views of the city. But Olomouc is not just about the big landmarks; it's in the smaller details, too. The city is full of public art installations, quirky sculptures, and hidden murals that reflect its creative spirit. Wandering through the streets, I discovered vibrant cafes and independent galleries tucked between centuries-old buildings, each one offering a taste of the city's artistic soul. If you're into street art, make sure to check out the area around the Upper Square, where you can find murals painted on both public buildings and the sides of hidden alleys. It's a charming blend of old and new that makes Olomouc's art scene so dynamic.

After soaking up all the art and history, I found myself in need of a bit of relaxation and a good meal, which Olomouc certainly didn't disappoint on. The city's food scene offers a delightful mix of traditional Czech fare with modern twists. I dined at several excellent restaurants, but my favorite was "Svatováclavská Vinárna," a cozy wine cellar-style restaurant offering a fantastic selection of Czech wines paired with local dishes. The ambiance is warm and welcoming, with wooden beams and intimate lighting, making it the perfect place to unwind after a day of sightseeing. The menu is extensive, offering everything from hearty Czech stews to lighter vegetarian options, all made with fresh, locally-sourced ingredients. Prices are reasonable, with meals typically ranging from $10 to $20 per person. For a more contemporary experience, I highly recommend "Café La Fée," a modern café offering artisanal coffee, light bites, and delicious pastries. It's located just off the main square, making it an ideal spot for a break while exploring the city. The café's relaxed, bohemian vibe pairs perfectly with its great selection of freshly brewed coffee and cakes. I couldn't resist trying their chocolate mousse, which was rich and indulgent, the perfect pick-me-up during an afternoon stroll.

When it comes to accommodations, Olomouc offers a range of options that cater to different tastes and budgets. For a luxurious stay, I chose the "NH Collection Olomouc Congress" hotel, a contemporary hotel located in the city center. It offers spacious, comfortable rooms with all the amenities you'd expect from a high-end hotel. The hotel also has an excellent restaurant and wellness center, providing a relaxing retreat after a day of sightseeing. Rates at this hotel generally range from $90 to $160 per night, depending on the time of year. If you're looking for something more budget-friendly, "Hotel Arigone" is a great option. Located just a short walk from the city center, it offers cozy rooms with a homey feel. The hotel's breakfast is hearty, and the staff are friendly and eager to help with recommendations. Rates here usually fall between $50 and $80 per night, making it an affordable choice without sacrificing comfort.

Getting around Olomouc is easy, as the city's public transport network includes trams, buses, and taxis. I found it easiest to walk everywhere, given how compact the city center is, but for those looking to explore a bit further, the trams and buses run frequently and are a quick way to cover more ground. The city is also bicycle-friendly, with bike-sharing options available for those who prefer to cycle.

Day Trips to Karlštejn Castle and Kutná Hora

If you find yourself in Prague, you're in luck—two unforgettable day trips lie just a short distance from the city, offering a mix of history, beauty, and unique experiences. Karlštejn Castle and Kutná Hora each offer their own slice of Czech heritage, and having spent time in both, I can confidently say they're well worth the visit.

Let me start with Karlštejn Castle, a stunning Gothic fortress perched in the Bohemian countryside. About a 40-minute drive southwest from Prague, this medieval stronghold is one of the most iconic castles in the Czech Republic. I've been there a few times, and every visit feels like stepping back in time. The castle was originally built in the 14th century by Emperor Charles IV to house royal treasures, including the crown jewels. As I approached the castle, its towering stone walls and impressive gatehouse rose above the trees, and it immediately felt like I had entered a fairy tale. The castle's interior is just as impressive as its exterior. The highlight for me was the Chapel of the Holy Cross, a magnificent room adorned with intricate frescoes and 130 painted panels depicting scenes from the life of Christ. The chapel's role as a vault for royal treasures and relics adds a layer of mystery and grandeur to the experience. Touring Karlštejn takes a bit of time, especially if you opt for one of the guided tours, which are available in multiple languages. I highly recommend taking the "Grand Tour" if you have the time—it includes the most detailed access to the castle's rooms and the beautiful chapel.

Getting to Karlštejn is straightforward from Prague. The train ride from Prague's main station takes about 40 minutes, and from the Karlštejn train station, it's just a 20-minute walk up to the castle. If you're not in the mood for the walk, you can catch a local bus or even take a taxi. The train tickets are reasonably priced, typically ranging from $2 to $5 for a one-way ticket. When it comes to food and accommodation, there are a few cozy spots in Karlštejn to make your visit even more enjoyable. For a peaceful night's stay, I recommend Hotel Karlštejn (Sídliště 1, Karlštejn, Czech Republic, +420 311 672 101, www.hotelkarlstejn.cz). It's a charming hotel just a short walk from the castle, and the rooms are comfortable, with a rustic yet modern feel. Rates start around $50 per night, which is quite affordable considering the proximity to such a historical landmark. The hotel also has an onsite restaurant where you can enjoy traditional Czech dishes. I tried their svíčková (a beef dish served with creamy sauce) and was very pleased with the flavors.

If you're looking for something less formal, Restaurace U Adama (Karlštejn 26, Karlštejn, Czech Republic, +420 311 671 606, www.restauraceuadama.cz) offers a cozy atmosphere with great views of the countryside.

Their Czech beers are the perfect way to relax after a castle tour. The prices here are moderate, usually between $10 to $20 per person, depending on what you order.

Now, after a magical day at Karlštejn, you might want to head to Kutná Hora, about an hour's drive east of Prague. This charming town, once the center of silver mining, is a UNESCO World Heritage site. I visited Kutná Hora for its famous Sedlec Ossuary, or the "Bone Church," a macabre but fascinating chapel adorned with human bones. The moment I stepped inside, I was struck by the sight of skulls and bones arranged in intricate patterns across the walls, chandeliers, and even a massive coat of arms. It's an unusual and eerie experience, but it gives a haunting insight into the town's history, where the remains of tens of thousands of people were used to decorate the chapel in the 19th century. Aside from the Bone Church, Kutná Hora has other gems worth exploring, including the St. Barbara's Church, a

Gothic masterpiece that has stood for over 700 years. It's one of the most iconic landmarks in the Czech Republic, with its soaring spires and beautiful frescoes inside. I spent several hours walking around Kutná Hora, taking in the medieval architecture and the quaint streets, which felt like a living museum. Don't miss the Czech Museum of Silver, which provides a fascinating look into the town's mining history and even offers guided tours of an old silver mine.

The town is easy to reach from Prague by train, with a journey time of around 1 hour and 10 minutes from the main station. Once you arrive at the Kutná Hora train station, it's just a short bus ride or walk to the town center. Train tickets are about $3 to $6 one-way, making it an affordable option for a day trip. When it comes to accommodations in Kutná Hora, Hotel Garni Na Havlíčku (Havlíčkova 519, Kutná Hora, Czech Republic, +420 327 512 761, www.hotel-garni.cz) is a solid choice. It's a short walk from the town center, offering comfortable rooms at a very reasonable price. Rates are typically $50 to $75 per night. The hotel also serves a delicious buffet breakfast, and it's a peaceful place to relax after a day of sightseeing. If you're hungry after touring the town, Restaurace Dačický (Husova 60, Kutná Hora, Czech Republic, +420 327 512 079, www.dacicky.cz) is an excellent spot to try traditional Czech food. The restaurant is housed in a historic building, and the ambiance is cozy and welcoming. I had their roasted duck with sauerkraut and dumplings, which was delicious and filling. Expect to pay around $10 to $20 per person here, depending on your choice of dish.

CHAPTER 7

Lesser-Known Treasures

When most people think of the Czech Republic, they picture the grandeur of Prague's Old Town, the majestic Prague Castle, or perhaps the iconic Charles Bridge. But the Czech Republic is full of lesser-known treasures that truly capture the heart and soul of this fascinating country. As I wandered off the beaten path during my travels, I discovered a side of the Czech Republic that most tourists miss—the quiet, hidden gems that reveal a different kind of magic.

In this chapter, I'll take you on a journey through some of these lesser-known places, from the historic charm of Lesser Town and Vyšehrad, to the secluded cultural treasures tucked away in places like Bethlehem Chapel and Strahov Monastery. We'll also explore some of Prague's most tranquil courtyards, where you can escape the crowds and soak in the peace and beauty of this remarkable city. And if you're craving a bit of nature, I'll share some natural enclaves that are perfect for those seeking a break from the urban bustle. These are the spots that offer a deeper, more intimate experience of the Czech Republic—places that, I promise, will leave you with lasting memories far beyond the typical tourist attractions.

So, if you're ready to explore Prague and beyond like a local and discover its hidden corners, let's dive into these lesser-known treasures and uncover the parts of the Czech Republic that many visitors never get the chance to see.

Historical Walks: Exploring Lesser Town and Vyšehrad

When I first set foot in Prague, I was immediately drawn to its history, not just the grand buildings and famous landmarks, but the quiet corners that hold centuries of stories. Lesser Town (Malá Strana) and Vyšehrad, two of the city's most historic areas, are perfect places to take a step back in time and experience the quieter, more intimate side of Prague. I found that wandering these areas allowed me to uncover some of the city's richest history while escaping the bustle of the more tourist-heavy parts of town.

Lesser Town, which lies just below Prague Castle, is one of the city's most charming neighborhoods. As I walked its cobbled streets, it felt like I was stepping into a medieval painting. The buildings, with their warm, golden hues and Baroque facades, are a reminder of a Prague from another era. I particularly enjoyed walking along the picturesque Maltese Square (Náměstí Maltézské), where the impressive Maltese Church stands tall—a perfect example of Baroque architecture. If you're a fan of quiet, historic neighborhoods, Lesser Town is an essential stop. One of my favorite hidden gems in Lesser Town was the Church of St. Nicholas. As I entered, the opulence of the interior caught me by surprise—the gilded altars, the frescoed ceilings—it's a visual feast for anyone who appreciates Baroque art. What I didn't expect was the peaceful ambiance inside, despite its grandeur. It's a perfect example of how Lesser Town manages to blend beauty with calm, creating a special kind of atmosphere that's hard to find elsewhere in Prague.

From Lesser Town, I crossed the Vltava River to explore Vyšehrad. Perched on a hill overlooking the city, Vyšehrad isn't as crowded as Prague Castle, but the views it offers are just as spectacular. It's an ancient fort, but unlike the intimidating spires of the castle, Vyšehrad has a more relaxed vibe. As I wandered around, I came across the Basilica of St. Peter and St. Paul, with its striking neo-Gothic towers. The cemetery beside it is the final resting place of many famous Czechs, including composers Antonín Dvořák and Bedřich Smetana. What struck me about Vyšehrad was the sense of tranquility—it felt as though time slowed down here, offering the perfect escape from the city's fast-paced energy.

While exploring these areas, I found that Lesser Town and Vyšehrad are both easy to access and offer some great places to stay and dine. For a cozy, historic place to stay, I recommend the Hotel Golden Star in Lesser Town. It's located just a short walk from Prague Castle, so you can enjoy easy access to the sights but also retreat into a more peaceful area at the end of the day. The hotel offers elegant rooms with a blend of modern amenities and old-world charm. Expect to pay around $90–$130 per night, depending on the season. The hotel also serves a delicious breakfast, and the staff is incredibly helpful with recommendations for things to do in the area. For dining, you can't go wrong with a visit to U Malířů, a restaurant in Lesser Town that's been serving classic Czech fare for centuries. The atmosphere is warm and inviting, with wood-panelled walls and old paintings adorning the space. It's a fantastic place to try traditional dishes like Svíčková (beef in creamy sauce) and Czech dumplings, and the prices are reasonable—expect to pay around $20–$30 for a main dish. It's a great spot for a relaxed, memorable meal after a day of exploring.

If you're staying near Vyšehrad, I'd also recommend checking out Café Kampa, a charming spot by the river that serves coffee and light bites. It's a perfect place to unwind after a stroll along the fortifications. A coffee will set you back about $3–$5, and the outdoor seating area gives you a lovely view of the river and the city. Getting to these historic areas is easy. Lesser Town is well-connected by tram, with several stops near the Prague Castle, including the Malostranská stop (Tram #12, #20, #22). Vyšehrad can be reached by tram as well, with the Vyšehrad stop (Tram #7, #24) right at the base of the hill. Both areas are easily walkable from the city center, and while they're popular with tourists, they never feel overcrowded, which made my visits feel relaxed and unhurried.

So, if you're looking to experience Prague's history from a different perspective—away from the crowds and right in the heart of where it all started—Lesser Town and Vyšehrad are absolutely worth the visit. Whether you're marveling at the Baroque churches, soaking up the views, or just enjoying the peaceful atmosphere, these historic areas offer a perfect balance of culture, beauty, and serenity.

Off-the-Beaten Path Cultural Sites: Bethlehem Chapel and Strahov Monastery

During my time in Prague, I found that some of the city's most captivating cultural gems aren't the usual landmarks everyone flocks to. Instead, they are tucked away in quieter corners, offering a deeper and often more intimate look at the city's rich history. Two places that truly stood out to me were the Bethlehem Chapel and Strahov Monastery—two off-the-beaten-path sites that are a must-see for anyone wanting to dive deeper into Prague's cultural and religious past.

The Bethlehem Chapel, located in Prague's Old Town, isn't the easiest to find if you don't know where to look, but that's part of its charm. Walking through narrow, cobbled streets, I stumbled upon this medieval chapel, tucked between modern buildings as though the centuries had passed it by unnoticed. This little chapel is historically significant not just for its age but for its role in Czech religious and intellectual history. It was here, in the 14th century, that Jan Hus, one of the most important figures in Czech history, preached. Hus, a religious reformer who was a forerunner to Martin Luther, delivered his sermons in the chapel, challenging the Church's practices and beliefs. Standing in the small, simple space, I couldn't help but feel a sense of reverence for the movements that began here, which later had such a profound impact on both Czech and European history.

The chapel's interior is simple, almost stark, with its wooden beams and the low, humble ceilings. It's not grand or decorated like many of the city's larger churches, but there's something deeply powerful about its simplicity. When I visited, it wasn't crowded—just a few other travelers quietly taking in the history and the atmosphere. The chapel itself is a fascinating site for those interested in religious history or the Reformation, and it's a reminder of how Prague has always been a city of intellectual and cultural movements. Bethlehem Chapel is located on Betlémské náměstí in the Old Town, easily accessible by public transport. The nearest tram stop is Národní třída (lines #9, #14), and it's only a short walk from there.

On the other side of town, a visit to Strahov Monastery offers a completely different experience, yet one equally steeped in history and culture. Perched on a hill overlooking the city, Strahov Monastery is home to a rich religious tradition and is famous for its extraordinary library and the beautiful Baroque church. I made my way to the monastery from the Malostranské náměstí tram stop (lines #12, #20, #22), and the walk up to the site was a little strenuous, but the views over Prague made it well worth the effort. The monastery was founded in the 12th century by the Premonstratensian Order, and while it has seen much change over the years, it still retains much of its original grandeur. One of the things that struck me most about Strahov was its library. The Strahov Library is a true hidden treasure—an 18th-century Baroque masterpiece filled with thousands of old books. I spent what felt like hours admiring the rows upon rows of leather-bound volumes and ornate decorations. The atmosphere inside was serene, and I couldn't help but imagine scholars poring over these same books hundreds of years ago. The library is split into two rooms: the Philosophical Hall and the Theological Hall, each with its own unique character. The Philosophical Hall is particularly striking with its towering bookshelves and stunning ceiling frescoes that seem to stretch into the heavens.

Beyond the library, the monastery complex itself is home to a small museum with artifacts from its long history, and the Strahov Basilica is another highlight—its intricate frescoes and detailed Baroque design left me in awe. It's a quieter place to explore compared to some of Prague's more famous attractions, and the peaceful atmosphere makes it easy to lose track of time as you wander the grounds and take in the surroundings. If you're looking for a place to stay while visiting Strahov, there's the Hotel Monastery, which is just a short walk from the monastery itself. The hotel is quaint and offers comfortable accommodations with modern amenities, and the location couldn't be better for accessing both Strahov and the rest of Prague. The rooms are reasonably priced, typically ranging from $80 to $120 a night, and the hotel staff is very welcoming, making it an ideal spot for a relaxed stay in a more tranquil part of Prague. The restaurant inside offers classic Czech dishes at affordable prices, and it's a nice place to unwind after a day of sightseeing.

For dining near the Bethlehem Chapel, I recommend visiting Café Louvre, a historic café that has been a favorite of locals and visitors alike since 1902. It's just a short walk from the chapel, and it's the perfect spot for a coffee or a traditional Czech pastry like koláče. The café serves hearty Czech dishes as well, and the prices are reasonable, with a typical meal ranging from $10 to $20.

Both Bethlehem Chapel and Strahov Monastery provide fascinating glimpses into Prague's lesser-known, but deeply rich, cultural and religious heritage. They're a welcome change from the busy tourist spots, offering a quieter, more reflective experience. Whether you're a history lover, an architecture enthusiast, or just someone who enjoys discovering hidden parts of a city, these two sites are sure to leave a lasting impression. The history here feels alive, and the peaceful atmosphere allows you to connect with the past in a way that larger attractions sometimes can't.

Discover Prague's Secluded Courtyards, and Natural Enclaves

During my time in Prague, I discovered that the city has a charm that extends far beyond its well-known landmarks. While most visitors flock to the Old Town Square or Charles Bridge, there's something uniquely captivating about wandering through Prague's quieter, hidden spaces—its secluded courtyards and natural enclaves. These spots, tucked away from the usual crowds, offer a peaceful escape and a chance to see a different side of the city's history and beauty.

One of my favorite experiences was exploring the courtyards scattered throughout the city, each offering its own slice of tranquility. These courtyards are often surrounded by old buildings, some of which date back centuries. What I found so remarkable about them is how they retain a sense of serenity and timelessness despite the bustling city that surrounds them. I spent a lovely afternoon in the courtyard of the Church of St.

James, for instance. Hidden down a narrow alley off the busy street, the church courtyard was surprisingly quiet, with only a few people strolling through. The cool shade of the trees, the scent of fresh flowers, and the occasional distant sound of a street musician created an almost meditative atmosphere. This is the type of place where I could just sit for hours, sipping coffee from a nearby café, and let the city pass by.

Another courtyard that I highly recommend is the one behind the Wallenstein Palace. This place is a hidden gem right in the heart of the city, yet so many people overlook it. The palace itself is grand and impressive, but the real treasure is the peaceful garden and courtyard that lie behind its walls. The garden is impeccably manicured, with sculptures, fountains, and shaded areas where you can relax. I wandered through it on a warm afternoon, marveling at the well-kept hedges and the tranquil pond in the middle. The fact that this courtyard is so close to Prague's bustling city center, yet feels worlds away, makes it even more special. It's a great spot to pause and reflect or simply enjoy the silence away from the city noise.

Prague's natural enclaves are another aspect of the city that surprised me. Despite being a major European capital, Prague is home to plenty of green spaces, parks, and natural reserves that feel far removed from urban life. One of my favorite spots to connect with nature was the Petřín Hill. I took the funicular up the hill, and once at the top, I was greeted by a sprawling park with beautiful gardens, forests, and sweeping views of the city. As I wandered through the park, it felt as though I had stepped into a secret garden. The peaceful atmosphere, combined with the stunning panoramic views of Prague below, made this a truly magical experience. It's the kind of place where you can hike up a hill and find yourself lost in nature, with nothing but the sound of birds and rustling leaves to keep you company. Another hidden natural gem in Prague is the Vltava

Riverbanks. While most people enjoy walking along the river near the main bridges, there are other, quieter stretches where you can truly enjoy the natural beauty of the city. I took a walk along the riverbank near the Vyšehrad fortress and discovered a small, secluded park right on the water. Here, I was surrounded by trees, wildflowers, and the gentle flow of the river. The atmosphere was peaceful, and I felt like I had found a tiny oasis in the middle of the city. I also stumbled upon a small, charming café tucked into the greenery where I stopped for a coffee and enjoyed the view.

I also recommend exploring the gardens surrounding the Prague Castle. While the castle itself is a well-known attraction, the gardens are often overlooked by tourists. These gardens, which date back to the 16th century, offer an impressive mix of landscaped beauty and historic architecture. Walking through the gardens, I encountered elegant fountains, manicured hedges, and even a hidden vineyard, all with spectacular views of the city below. If you're looking to truly experience the natural beauty of Prague while escaping the crowds, the Divoká Šárka nature reserve is a must-visit. This nature reserve is located a bit farther from the city center, but it's well worth the trip. It offers hiking trails through rugged terrain, lush forests, and even swimming spots in the summer. I spent a few hours here, walking through the forest and stopping to take in the quiet, untouched beauty of the area. The only sounds I heard were the chirping of birds and the rustling of leaves in the breeze. It was the perfect way to recharge and connect with nature away from the city buzz.

What I love most about Prague is how these hidden courtyards and natural enclaves reveal the city's dual nature: a vibrant urban center brimming with history, but also a place where peace and solitude can be found just around the corner.

CHAPTER 8

Southern Bohemia

Southern Bohemia is a region that often feels like a well-kept secret in the Czech Republic—untouched, tranquil, and brimming with history. As I journeyed through this picturesque part of the country, I quickly realized why it's a favorite among those looking for a more relaxed, yet equally fascinating, side of the Czech Republic. Unlike the bustling streets of Prague, Southern Bohemia offers a slower pace, where history is not just found in museums, but in the very stones of its towns and castles. In this chapter, I'll be taking you on a tour of some of the region's most remarkable sites, starting with the fairy-tale Český Krumlov Castle, a place that feels almost as though it has stepped out of a storybook. From there, we'll venture to the grand Hluboká Castle, an architectural marvel with a rich history that's well worth exploring. For those who prefer the outdoors, we'll explore the Lipno Reservoir, a serene body of water perfect for outdoor activities, and the nearby Šumava National Park, a paradise for hikers with trails that wind through lush forests and across rolling hills. Southern Bohemia is a region that invites you to slow down, step off the beaten path, and really absorb the beauty and culture of the Czech countryside. Whether you're a history buff, an outdoor enthusiast, or simply someone looking to escape the crowds, this part of the country has something to offer. What I found most striking is how each place seems to tell its own unique story—whether it's a castle perched on a hill, a quiet lake, or a rugged mountain trail. And trust me, once you set foot here, you'll find it hard to leave.

Historical Sites: Český Krumlov Castle and Hluboká Castle

When I first visited Český Krumlov Castle, I was taken aback by the sheer size and beauty of the place. Nestled in the heart of Český Krumlov, a UNESCO World Heritage town in Southern Bohemia, this castle complex is a true gem that feels almost suspended in time. As I walked through its narrow cobbled streets, surrounded by medieval buildings, I couldn't help but imagine life here centuries ago, when it was home to some of the most powerful families in the region.

The castle itself is a massive structure, spanning over 10 acres, and boasts a fascinating blend of architectural styles—Gothic, Renaissance, and Baroque. The thing that stood out to me was the way the castle seemed to reflect the history of this town. From the old courtyards and halls to the impressive Baroque theatre (which is still in use today for performances), every corner of the castle tells a story. The highlight for me was the

Castle Tower, which offers a stunning view over the town, the Vltava River, and the surrounding hills. The castle is easily accessible, located just a short walk from the main square in Český Krumlov. If you're coming from Prague, it's about a two-and-a-half-hour drive or a comfortable two-hour train ride to the town. Once there, it's easy to get to the castle by following the signs or taking a quick taxi.

Not too far from Český Krumlov, Hluboká Castle stands as another magnificent historical site, albeit with a slightly different character. When I first laid eyes on this castle, I was struck by its resemblance to the fairy-tale castles of Germany. Built in the mid-13th century, the castle has undergone multiple renovations over the centuries, culminating in its current form—a stunning Gothic Revival style that looks like it was plucked straight from a storybook. Unlike Český Krumlov, which retains much of its medieval feel, Hluboká feels grander and more polished, with sprawling gardens and meticulously manicured grounds that invite you to take a leisurely stroll. Inside, the castle is equally impressive, with lavishly decorated rooms, opulent furniture, and fascinating exhibits showcasing the history of the Czech aristocracy. One of the highlights of my visit was the grand dining hall, which felt as though it could easily host a royal banquet. To get there, Hluboká is located just a 15-minute drive from České Budějovice, which is about two hours from Prague by car or train. If you're in the area, it's definitely worth visiting both castles as they each offer something unique—Český Krumlov's medieval charm and Hluboká's fairy-tale elegance.

Whether you're an architecture lover, a history enthusiast, or just someone who appreciates beauty, these two castles should be at the top of your list when exploring Southern Bohemia.

Discovering the Lipno Reservoir

When I first visited the Lipno Reservoir, I wasn't sure what to expect. Tucked away in the southern corner of the Czech Republic, this vast body of water surrounded by the lush forests of the Šumava region felt like a well-kept secret. As I walked along the shoreline, I was immediately struck by the peacefulness of the place. The reservoir spans over 40 square kilometers, and its shimmering surface seemed to stretch on forever. It's hard to believe that a man-made creation like this could feel so natural. The Lipno Reservoir was built in the 1950s as part of a hydroelectric project, but today it's one of the most popular spots in Southern Bohemia for both locals and tourists seeking a mix of outdoor activities and relaxation.

One of the highlights of my time there was a boat ride on the reservoir. The gentle waves rocked the small boat as we made our way across the water, surrounded by dense forests and small inlets that felt almost untouched. The surrounding area is full of well-maintained hiking and cycling paths, so I took advantage of the beautiful weather to explore on foot. Whether you're into cycling, hiking, or just taking in the scenery, the surroundings offer a variety of routes to suit all levels. The views of the water against the backdrop of the forested hills are breathtaking, and there's something quite special about the silence, broken only by the sound of birds and the occasional ripple of water.

I also discovered that Lipno Reservoir is a hub for watersports, particularly in the summer months. I saw kayaks, paddleboards, and even windsurfers gliding across the water. If you're looking for a more leisurely experience, there are plenty of places to rent a small boat or even take a guided tour of the reservoir to learn about its history and ecological significance. And when I needed a break, I found a charming lakeside café where I could sit, relax, and enjoy a traditional Czech meal while taking in the views. Getting to Lipno is surprisingly easy, despite the reservoir being set in such a tranquil, remote area. It's located about 25 kilometers from the town of Český Krumlov, which makes it easily accessible by car. The drive takes you through picturesque rural landscapes, and if you're coming from Český Krumlov, it's a very pleasant 30-minute journey.

For those who don't have a car, there are also bus routes that run regularly between Český Krumlov and Lipno, making it easy to get there by public transport. Once you arrive, you'll find that the area is well-developed for tourism, with plenty of accommodation options ranging from cozy hotels to lakeside cabins.

Scenic Routes: Hiking in Šumava National Park

When I first set foot in Šumava National Park, I wasn't sure what to expect. I had heard about its rugged beauty and vast forests, but nothing could have prepared me for the experience of hiking through its diverse landscapes. Located in the southern part of the Czech Republic, Šumava is a paradise for nature lovers, offering some of the most scenic routes in the country. As I walked along its winding trails, I felt as if I was stepping into a living painting, where every turn revealed a new vista—towering trees, serene lakes, and wildflower-filled meadows.

One of the things I loved most about hiking in Šumava is the variety of landscapes it offers. The park is part of the Šumava mountain range, which borders Austria and Germany, and it's one of the largest protected areas in Central Europe. The terrain can be challenging in some spots, but there are trails for every level of hiker. On one of my first hikes, I found myself following a gentle path that meandered through dense pine forests, where the scent of the trees mixed with the freshness of the air. The forest floor was soft with moss, and I could hear the rustling of small animals in the underbrush. As I walked deeper into the park, I found myself at the edge of a sparkling lake, its waters reflecting the sky above like a mirror.

For a more challenging adventure, I decided to tackle some of the higher trails, which lead to panoramic viewpoints offering sweeping views of the surrounding mountains and valleys. One of my favorite routes took me up to the highest point in the park, the Velký Bor hill, where I could see for miles across the Czech countryside, the distant peaks of the Alps visible on clear days. The trail was a bit steeper, but the reward at the top was well worth it. From there, I could spot tiny villages nestled in the valleys and rivers winding through the landscape below. The park also features well-marked paths that lead through ancient forests, past glacial lakes, and along tranquil rivers. Some of the trails even pass through historical sites, where you can learn about the region's past, including its traditional wooden villages and the remnants of old mills. I walked a section of the "Bohemian Forest Trail," a long-distance route that stretches for over 200 kilometers and showcases the park's rich natural beauty. Along the way, I passed through dense thickets of spruce trees and open meadows dotted with wildflowers. It felt like stepping into another world—a place where time seemed to slow down and nature took center stage.

What struck me the most about Šumava was how untouched it feels. The park is a haven for wildlife, and I was lucky enough to spot deer, wild boar, and even an eagle soaring high above. The quiet is something I hadn't experienced in a long time. Even though the park attracts plenty of visitors, it never felt crowded. There's a peaceful solitude here that allows you to truly connect with nature. Getting to Šumava is easier than I thought. From Prague, you can take a direct bus or train to the town of Český Krumlov, which is located near the park's entrance. From there, you can take a local bus or rent a car to reach the trailheads. If you prefer driving, the journey from Prague to Šumava takes about two and a half hours, and the roads are well-maintained, making the drive pleasant. Once inside the park, getting around is simple, with well-marked trails and plenty of signs to guide you along the way.

If you're planning on staying in the area, there are several charming guesthouses and hotels in the nearby towns, many of which offer cozy accommodations and local Czech cuisine. I stayed in a small village near the park and found it to be the perfect base for my hiking adventures. The locals were incredibly welcoming, and I had the chance to enjoy hearty meals after long days of hiking, including traditional Czech dishes like svíčková (a creamy beef stew) and knedlíky (dumplings).

Heading into the mountains, the Czech Republic offers a variety of ski resorts that are perfect for winter sports enthusiasts. The Špindlerův Mlýn Ski Resort stands out as a prime destination. Located in the heart of the Krkonoše Mountains, it provides a range of slopes suitable for all skill levels. The resort features modern facilities and stunning mountain views, making it a popular choice for both skiing and snowboarding. The resort is accessible by bus from Prague, which takes about two hours and drops you directly in the resort area.

CHAPTER 9

Northern Bohemia

When I first ventured into Northern Bohemia, I quickly realized how different it felt from the rest of the Czech Republic. This region, often overshadowed by the bustling cities like Prague, holds a raw beauty and a rich history that can leave you in awe. It's a place where nature and culture intertwine, offering a range of experiences from dramatic landscapes to poignant historical sites. If you've ever wanted to step off the well-worn tourist trail and explore a region that feels less touched by time, Northern Bohemia is where you should be.

One of the first places I found myself drawn to was Liberec, a charming city nestled at the foot of the Jizera Mountains. With its cool, almost alpine vibe, Liberec is a hidden gem that combines old-world charm with modern attractions. The city's proud history is reflected in the architecture—grand buildings, colorful town squares, and its famous Ještěd Tower, which seems to pierce the sky. From here, the Jizera Mountains stretch out in every direction, offering endless opportunities for outdoor exploration. Whether you're hiking, biking, or just strolling through the rolling hills and dense forests, there's a sense of serenity that makes this area feel like a peaceful retreat.

But the region has more to offer than just natural beauty. I was deeply moved when I visited Terezín, a town with a dark history but an important story to tell. The Terezín Memorial is one of the most poignant sites in the Czech Republic, a place that serves as a reminder of the horrors of the Holocaust. Walking through the former garrison town, I couldn't help but reflect on the lives lost here during World War II. The memorial's stark buildings and haunting exhibits tell a story of resilience and survival, and it's a place that stays with you long after you leave. For anyone who enjoys the outdoors, Northern Bohemia also boasts the stunning Bohemian Paradise, a UNESCO Global Geopark filled with sandstone rock formations, hidden caves, and medieval castles. I spent a day here exploring the rocky paths that lead you past towering spires and through lush forests. The sheer variety of landscapes—jagged cliffs, quiet valleys, and peaceful meadows—felt like a journey through nature's finest artwork.

Perhaps the most breathtaking of all the sights is Saxon Switzerland National Park, just over the border in Germany. But don't be fooled by the name—it's every bit as enchanting on the Czech side, where dramatic cliffs and gorges offer a paradise for hikers and photographers. I spent hours wandering through the park, often feeling as though I was walking through a fairy tale. The sweeping vistas, the lush green valleys, and the unique rock formations—especially the famous

Bastei Bridge—make it a must-visit for anyone in the area.

This chapter will guide you through these experiences, sharing not only the best places to see but also how to fully immerse yourself in the culture and natural wonders of Northern Bohemia. Whether you're keen to learn about history, hike through pristine landscapes, or simply take in the beauty of a region that's a little off the beaten path, Northern Bohemia offers it all. I can't wait to share more of what I discovered—so let's dive in and explore the hidden treasures that await in this remarkable corner of the Czech Republic.

Coastal Delights: Liberec and the Jizera Mountains

When I first visited Liberec and the Jizera Mountains, I was struck by how different the region felt compared to the more popular tourist spots in the Czech Republic. Liberec, a city tucked in the far north, near the borders with Poland and Germany, offers a surprisingly diverse mix of history, culture, and natural beauty. It's not as widely known as Prague or Český Krumlov, but it's definitely a place that will steal your heart once you give it a chance.

Liberec is the Czech Republic's fifth-largest city, but it feels much more like a charming town than a bustling metropolis. The city is best known for its striking mix of 20th-century architecture, including the iconic Ještěd Tower. This tower, shaped like a futuristic spire, rises over 1,000 meters above sea level, offering sweeping views of the surrounding region. When I took the cable car up to Ještěd, I was absolutely mesmerized by the panoramic vistas—on clear days, you can even spot the peaks of the Krkonoš Mountains to the north. The tower also houses a hotel and restaurant, so you can enjoy a meal while taking in the view. Liberec itself is a perfect base for exploring the Jizera Mountains, which are just a short drive or train ride away. The Jizera Mountains, part of the Czech-Polish border region, are a haven for nature lovers and outdoor enthusiasts. While the Krkonoš Mountains often get more attention, I found the Jizera range to be just as beautiful, with far fewer crowds. The mountains are covered with dense forests, and there are plenty of well-marked trails that make hiking a true pleasure. Whether you're into leisurely walks or more challenging treks, you'll find something that suits your level.

One of the things I loved most about hiking here is the absolute peace and quiet you'll experience. The trails are often solitary, with only the occasional chirp of birds or the rustle of leaves breaking the silence. One standout trail I did was the "Jizera Ridge Trail," which takes you along the ridgeline and offers spectacular views of the valleys below. It's a relatively easy hike, but the rewards are more than worth it—especially when you come across the charming wooden cottages that dot the landscape.

For something even more off-the-beaten-path, the Jizera Mountains also have a rich history tied to the local community. I stumbled upon a few quiet, remote villages where time seemed to stand still. These areas were once part of the Sudetenland and are steeped in history that not many people know about. You can learn a lot just by walking through these towns, taking in the old architecture, and chatting with locals who have lived there for generations. Getting to Liberec is fairly simple. From Prague, it's about a two-hour train ride north, with regular departures from the main train station. You can also take a bus from Prague, but the train is faster and more comfortable. Once in Liberec, the city is small enough that it's easy to explore on foot or by public transport. The Jizera Mountains are just a short ride away by local bus, and once you're out in the mountains, you'll find that hiking paths are well connected by public transportation or taxis.

If you're a nature lover looking for an authentic experience in a less touristy part of the Czech Republic, Liberec and the Jizera Mountains will likely become a highlight of your trip. From the scenic views atop Ještěd to the tranquil trails of the Jizera Ridge, this part of the country offers both relaxation and adventure in equal measure. And while it's not as packed with tourists as Prague or other well-known cities, I found that only added to its charm. The beauty of the landscape and the laid-back vibe of the region made me feel like I was uncovering something special, tucked away in the Czech Republic's northern corner.

Terezín Memorial and Bohemian Paradise

Visiting Terezín Memorial was one of the most moving and humbling experiences of my travels through the Czech Republic. Located about an hour's drive north of Prague, Terezín is a small town that carries a heavy history. During World War II, it was transformed into a Nazi concentration camp, serving as a holding facility for thousands of Jews before they were sent to other camps or extermination centers. Today, it's a place of remembrance, reflection, and education—a somber but necessary part of understanding the darker chapters of European history.

The memorial itself is split into two main sites: the Small Fortress and the Ghetto. The Small Fortress was used primarily for political prisoners and has a stark, chilling atmosphere. The walls of the fortress are lined with stories of hardship, resistance, and survival. As I walked through the cold, stone corridors, it was hard not to feel the weight of the countless lives that passed through here. The most powerful part for me was the old prison cells, which had been preserved in their original state. These grim spaces offer an intimate glimpse into the suffering endured by those held here. I found it emotionally intense, but it's an important part of understanding the legacy of Terezín.

The Ghetto area of Terezín is just as poignant, though in a different way. Once a thriving community, it was transformed into a place of confinement, overcrowded with families, artists, and intellectuals who had been rounded up by the Nazis. Despite the hardship, the residents found ways to create art, theater, and music as acts of resistance. The Ghetto Museum is home to exhibits that document the lives of these people, their forced relocation, and the creative ways they kept their humanity amidst inhumane conditions. One exhibit that stuck with me was a collection of drawings made by children in Terezín. Seeing the art made by young hands, so raw and innocent, struck me deeply. It's a reminder of how, even in the face of unimaginable terror, people clung to what they could—their creativity, their culture, and their spirit. To get to Terezín, I took a train from Prague to the nearby town of Lovosice and then hopped onto a local bus that took me straight to the memorial. It's relatively simple to reach by public transport, but renting a car would offer more flexibility, especially if you're planning to visit multiple sites in the region. Once you arrive, the memorial is well-marked and easy to navigate. There's also a very informative visitor center where you can gather maps and more background information about the history of the site.

After reflecting on Terezín, I wanted to explore something that felt a little lighter, so I made my way to Bohemian Paradise, a stunning national park about an hour away by car. Bohemian Paradise is often hailed as one of the most beautiful natural areas in the Czech Republic, and it truly lives up to the hype. It's a place where dense forests, towering rock formations, and medieval castles meet, creating a dramatic and picturesque landscape. One of the highlights for me was hiking through the Prachov Rocks, a maze of sandstone towers that rise high above the surrounding forest. The view from the top was breathtaking, and as I stood there, I couldn't help but feel a sense of peace after the weight of Terezín.

What makes Bohemian Paradise special is that it's not just about the natural beauty; it's also home to a number of well-preserved castles and ruins. While hiking, I stumbled upon a few ruins, including the towering remains of Trosky Castle, which stands as a dramatic silhouette against the sky. This castle was built in the 14th century and was strategically positioned to oversee the entire region. Exploring its ruins felt like stepping back in time, and the view from the top, looking out over the valley, was one I'll never forget. Getting to Bohemian Paradise is easy if you have access to a car, but you can also reach the park by train and bus from nearby towns like Turnov. The park is filled with well-marked hiking trails, many of which are suitable for all levels of hikers. For a more laid-back experience, I recommend taking a leisurely walk through the forests or around the ponds. The natural beauty of the area is truly remarkable, and it offers a refreshing contrast to the historical gravity of Terezín.

Both Terezín Memorial and Bohemian Paradise are worth visiting for different reasons. Terezín is a profound, sobering experience that offers insight into the darkest chapters of history, while Bohemian Paradise is a restorative escape into nature. Together, these places show the full spectrum of human experience—both the depths of suffering and the heights of beauty. If you're in the Czech Republic, I highly recommend setting aside time for both.

Nature Observations: Saxon Switzerland National Park

Saxon Switzerland National Park, located just across the border from the Czech Republic into Germany, is a gem that completely captivated me during my time in the region. Often overshadowed by its more famous counterparts, this park is one of Europe's most dramatic natural landscapes. It's a place where nature seems to have sculpted the land into something extraordinary—towering sandstone cliffs, deep valleys, and lush forests make it feel like something straight out of a fairy tale. As I hiked through its trails, I found myself constantly in awe of the sheer scale and beauty of the landscape.

The park is named after the region's distinctive sandstone rock formations that resemble the jagged spires of a gothic cathedral, making it look almost otherworldly. From the moment I entered the park, I felt like I had stepped into a place frozen in time, with the rich greenery, flowing rivers, and the ever-present sandstone cliffs watching over me. One of the first places I visited was the Bastei Bridge, which is one of the park's most iconic landmarks. This bridge, built in the 19th century, offers breathtaking views over the Elbe River below, winding through a landscape dotted with the towering rocks that give the area its name. It's a spot where the dramatic cliffs meet the winding river, creating a postcard-perfect scene that you can't help but stop and stare at for what feels like hours. Standing on the bridge, with the wind in my face and the rocks looming around me, I felt like I was on top of the world.

Getting to Saxon Switzerland from the Czech Republic is easier than you might think. While the park is technically in Germany, the Czech side of the border provides access to some of its trails. If you're starting from Prague, you can easily take a bus or train to the town of Děčín, which is located on the Czech side of the park, just a short distance from the main trails. From Děčín, you can catch a bus or train to the nearby village of Hřensko, a popular gateway to the park. The journey is relatively straightforward, and if you're traveling by car, the drive is scenic in itself, winding through the Bohemian countryside and into the park's rolling hills. Once you arrive, you'll find that the park's trails are clearly marked and accessible, making it easy to explore even if you're not an experienced hiker.

What I loved about Saxon Switzerland is that it offers a variety of hiking trails, ranging from easy walks to more challenging climbs, making it perfect for anyone looking to connect with nature. On one of my hikes, I ventured up to the Königstein Fortress, which sits high atop a hill, offering panoramic views of the surrounding valleys and rock formations. The fortress itself is fascinating, with its long history dating back to the 16th century, but the real magic is in the view from the top. I stood there for a while, taking it all in—feeling small in the face of such grandeur, yet deeply connected to the earth beneath me. Another hike that stood out was the Pravčická Brána, or the Pravčice Gate, which is one of the largest natural sandstone arches in Europe. The arch, which spans a dramatic gorge, looks like something from a fantasy film, with its sweeping curves and rugged texture. Hiking up to the viewpoint was a bit of a challenge, but the sight of the arch from the top was worth every step. It felt surreal to be standing in front of such a natural wonder, and I found myself just staring at it for several minutes, soaking in its beauty. From here, you can catch glimpses of the distant Czech landscape, with its rolling hills and forests stretching out as far as the eye can see.

Aside from hiking, Saxon Switzerland is a great place for nature lovers to observe wildlife. The park is home to a variety of species, including wild boar, deer, and numerous bird species, which I spotted from time to time as I wandered the trails. The forests are filled with life, and every turn offers a new sight or sound—whether it's the call of a bird echoing through the trees or the rustle of leaves as something small scurries past. If you're an avid birdwatcher, you'll be in your element here, as the park is home to a rich variety of birds, including the peregrine falcon, which I was lucky enough to spot soaring high above the cliffs.

Saxon Switzerland also has a special charm in the off-season. While the summer months can see a lot of visitors, if you can manage to visit in the spring or fall, you'll find the park to be a quieter, more peaceful place to explore. I visited during the fall, and the landscape was ablaze with autumn colors—reds, yellows, and oranges creating a vibrant canvas that only added to the park's magic. The trails, which are already quite peaceful, feel even more intimate during these times, and you can spend hours walking through the forest, completely enveloped in nature.

CHAPTER 10

Central Bohemia

As I journeyed through Central Bohemia, I found myself continually amazed by the rich variety of experiences it offers, from historical landmarks to vibrant local traditions. The heart of the Czech Republic, this region is home to a perfect blend of discovery, culture, and heritage. In this chapter, I'll take you through some of the most captivating spots that Central Bohemia has to offer—places that tell stories from the past while remaining full of life today.

One of the first places that truly caught my attention was the Aviation Museum Kbely, just outside of Prague. Located in the quiet suburb of Kbely, this museum is a hidden gem for anyone with even a passing interest in aviation. As I wandered through the hangars, I was struck by how well-preserved the collection of aircraft was, from early pioneers of flight to Cold War-era jets. For aviation enthusiasts, it's a dream come true, with each plane carrying its own unique history, and I found myself spending hours there, learning about the Czech Republic's pivotal role in aviation history. But it's not just for aviation buffs—if you have an appreciation for engineering or simply enjoy marveling at large machines, this museum offers a fascinating look at both the beauty and the practicality of flight.

After soaking in the stories of the skies, I headed to one of the most eerie yet intriguing sites in the Czech Republic—the Bone Church of Sedlec. This small chapel, located just outside of Kutná Hora, holds a mysterious and somewhat macabre allure. As soon as I walked through the door, I was struck by the sight of thousands of human bones artfully arranged into chandeliers, pyramids, and intricate designs. The church, which dates back to the 14th century, serves as a solemn reminder of both life and death, and it's a place that leaves a lasting impression. For me, it was one of those moments where you feel both awe and reverence, as you try to take in the history and significance of the space.

And then there's Pilsen, a city known not only for its world-famous beer but also for its deeply-rooted local traditions and vibrant celebrations. When I visited, I was lucky enough to experience firsthand the town's rich history in beer brewing. Pilsen isn't just about drinking beer—it's about immersing yourself in a way of life that has been brewing for centuries. Local festivals celebrate traditional crafts and culinary delights, and I was invited to watch artisans at work, creating everything from glassware to handwoven textiles. Whether it's enjoying a local beer festival or simply exploring the old town, Pilsen has a warmth and charm that makes you feel instantly welcome. In the coming pages, I'll share more details about these unforgettable places and experiences, offering tips on how to make the most of your time in Central Bohemia. Whether you're fascinated by aviation, intrigued by history, or eager to discover the region's local crafts, this chapter will provide you with everything you need to explore the heart of the Czech Republic in a meaningful way. Central Bohemia is not just a place to visit—it's a place to connect with the past, the present, and the culture of this beautiful region.

Discovery and Learning: Aviation Museum Kbely

I'll never forget the day I decided to visit the Aviation Museum in Kbely, just on the outskirts of Prague. It's not your typical tourist destination, and that's exactly what made it stand out. Located in the Kbely district, northeast of the city center, the museum is housed in an old airbase, and as soon as I stepped inside, I was transported back in time. This museum, known officially as the Military History Institute Prague, is an absolute treasure trove of aviation history, especially for anyone like me who has even the slightest interest in aircraft.

The museum is not just a static collection of planes; it's a living, breathing testament to Czech aviation, spanning decades of technological advancements and wartime history. The first thing that struck me as I entered the large hangar was the sheer variety of aircraft on display. I had expected a few old planes, maybe some jets, but this was far beyond that. From early biplanes that looked almost fragile, to sleek Cold War-era fighters, to the unmistakable silhouette of the MiG-21, the museum offers a fascinating glimpse into the evolution of aviation in the Czech Republic.

Each plane tells its own story. I found myself drawn to the vintage Czechoslovak-made aircraft, such as the Aero L-39 Albatros, a trainer jet that's still used in some parts of the world today. The level of detail in the restoration is impressive, and walking around the planes, I couldn't help but imagine the stories these machines could tell. The museum does a fantastic job of contextualizing these aircraft within their historical significance. There are plenty of well-written descriptions, plus the museum's staff are passionate about sharing their knowledge, which makes the experience even more enriching. What I found truly special was how much effort has been made to bring the history to life. There are multimedia displays, photos, and even uniforms that give you insight into the people behind the machines. I remember reading about Czech aviators who risked their lives during World War II, flying alongside the Allies in the fight against the Axis powers. It wasn't just about the planes—it was about the bravery, the innovation, and the struggles that shaped the course of history.

Getting to the museum was surprisingly easy. Kbely is well-connected to the center of Prague, and I hopped on a bus from the Černý Most metro station (Line B). The trip was quick, taking just under 30 minutes, and once I got off, it was a short walk to the museum. There's also ample parking for those driving from elsewhere in the Czech Republic, and the area itself is quite peaceful, far from the hustle and bustle of Prague's busy tourist spots.

The Enigmatic Bone Church of Sedlec

The Bone Church of Sedlec—officially known as the Sedlec Ossuary—is one of the most unique and thought-provoking sites I've ever visited in the Czech Republic. Located in the small town of Kutná Hora, about an hour's train ride from Prague, this church holds a strange, eerie beauty that I wasn't quite prepared for when I first set foot inside. It's a place where history, art, and mortality come together in an unexpectedly striking way.

The Sedlec Ossuary is unlike anything you'll find elsewhere. It's a chapel adorned with the bones of tens of thousands of people. And I mean adorned—we're not talking about just a few scattered remains here and there. The bones are intricately arranged into chandeliers, coats of arms, and even large pyramids, creating a macabre yet oddly fascinating display. When I first entered the chapel, I was struck by how the light filtered through the high windows, casting soft shadows on the bone structures that decorated the walls. At first, I was unsure whether to feel awe or unease. But as I walked through, I began to appreciate the artistry behind it all.

The story behind this eerie display starts in the 13th century. The abbey of Sedlec, situated just outside Kutná Hora, was one of the most important religious sites in the region. When an abbot returned from the Holy Land in 1278, he brought back some earth from Jerusalem, which he sprinkled over the abbey's cemetery. This made the cemetery a highly desirable burial ground, attracting people from all over Europe. By the time the Black Death swept through in the 14th century, the number of bodies buried here had grown so large that the cemetery became overcrowded. In the 16th century, a Gothic chapel was built on the site, and it wasn't until the late 18th century, when the area was restructured, that the bones of the deceased were unearthed and arranged in the manner we see today. A woodcarver named František Rint was hired to organize the bones, and he created the intricate decorations we now recognize as the signature of the Sedlec Ossuary. As I wandered around the chapel, the detailed arrangements of skulls and bones were nothing short of mesmerizing. I remember being particularly taken by the large chandelier suspended from the ceiling, which consists of a vast array of bones—skulls, femurs, and other bones—strung together in a twisted, circular formation. It's difficult to describe the mixture of emotions this artwork evokes. On one hand, it's undeniably beautiful in its craftsmanship. On the other hand, it's an uncomfortable reminder of the fragility of life and the countless souls who once walked the earth.

Visiting the Bone Church of Sedlec is an easy trip from Prague. I took a direct train from Prague's main station, which took about an hour and was a relaxing ride through the Czech countryside. Once in Kutná Hora, the ossuary is only about a

20-minute walk from the train station, or you can hop on a local bus for a quick ride. It's a compact site, and the entrance fee is modest, especially considering how thought-provoking the experience is.

The experience at the Bone Church isn't just about the bones—it's a reflection on life, death, and how people throughout history have coped with loss. Walking through this space, surrounded by the remains of so many, I felt a deep sense of connection to the past. It's a place that stays with you long after you leave, not only for its startling beauty but for its reminder of the fleeting nature of life. If you're in the Czech Republic, this is a stop that shouldn't be missed. It's an unforgettable experience, one that combines history, artistry, and reflection in a way that's unlike any other.

Local Celebrations and Traditional Crafts in Pilsen

Pilsen, a vibrant city in western Bohemia, is not just known for being the birthplace of Pilsner beer—it's also a hub of rich traditions and local celebrations that really offer you a glimpse into Czech culture. I had the chance to experience these firsthand, and the more I learned about the customs, the more I felt connected to the people and the land.

One of the most interesting aspects of Pilsen is how deeply rooted the city's traditions are in its everyday life. During my visit, I was fortunate enough to catch one of the local celebrations that seem to pop up throughout the year. Pilsen, like many Czech cities, has a deep connection to its agricultural roots, which translates into numerous festivals that celebrate the changing seasons, harvests, and the continuation of cultural practices passed down through generations. One of the most memorable celebrations I attended was the

Plzeňské Slávnosti—the Pilsen Festival. Held in the summer, this festival celebrates everything from Czech folk music and dances to food and, of course, the famous Pilsner beer. It's a local tradition, and what's remarkable is how it brings together the entire community. Walking through the streets, I was surrounded by the joyful sounds of folk bands, the clink of beer glasses, and the hearty laughter of families enjoying themselves. The festival also showcases traditional Czech crafts, with local artisans displaying their work in outdoor markets. I spent some time exploring the beautifully handmade ceramics, wood carvings, and embroidered textiles, which are such a key part of Czech craftsmanship.

I remember chatting with one artisan, a woman who had been creating pottery for over 40 years. She explained to me how the art of ceramics has been practiced in Pilsen for centuries, with roots in the medieval period. The local pottery often features intricate, colorful designs inspired by nature and local folklore, and it's clear that these traditions are taken very seriously. For visitors, it's not just about buying a souvenir—it's about appreciating the painstaking effort and dedication that goes into each piece. What struck me most, however, was how these celebrations are not just for tourists—they are deeply personal for the people of Pilsen. It's about celebrating their heritage, the things that define their culture, and sharing that pride with others. The Plzeňské Slávnosti felt like a communal experience, a time for the city to come together and honor its history and traditions. People of all ages were involved, whether they were performing folk dances or enjoying the local foods that make the city so unique.

In addition to the festivals, there are a number of places in Pilsen where traditional crafts are still alive and well. One afternoon, I visited the Pilsen Craft Brewery—which, of course, wasn't just about the beer. This brewery, like many others in the region, prides itself on using old-world brewing techniques that have been passed down through the generations. The process is almost a ritual here, with careful attention to detail and ingredients, some of which are sourced locally. Watching the brewers at work, I gained an appreciation not only for the famous Pilsner lager but also for the craftsmanship involved in making it.

Aside from beer-making, Pilsen is also known for its long-standing tradition of glassmaking, another craft that has defined the region for centuries. On a visit to a local glass factory, I saw how molten glass was shaped by hand into delicate, intricate pieces of art. The factory's artisans work with both traditional and modern methods, and it's fascinating to watch the entire process unfold. The glass pieces, which range from delicate ornaments to stunning chandeliers, are a perfect example of the combination of skill and artistry that defines the local culture.

For those looking to dive even deeper into Pilsen's traditions, visiting the Pilsen City Museum is a must. It offers insights into the city's history, from its medieval beginnings to the industrial age, and showcases a variety of local crafts, including those from the regions surrounding the city. Here, I was able to learn about how the customs of beer brewing, glassmaking, and pottery evolved over time, influenced by everything from royal patronage to the practical needs of the local population.

Getting to Pilsen is easy enough. It's about an hour's train ride from Prague, and once you're there, the city itself is compact and walkable, making it easy to explore the different areas where these crafts and celebrations take place.

CHAPTER 11

Western Bohemia

Western Bohemia is one of those regions of the Czech Republic that seems to weave together the threads of history, nature, and culture in ways that feel almost effortless. When I first arrived in this part of the country, I was struck by the variety of experiences on offer. From the historical significance of Cheb to the relaxing atmosphere of Karlovy Vary, and the tranquil beauty of Mariánské Lázně, each place told its own unique story.

Cheb, for example, feels like a step back in time. The town is steeped in military history, with its medieval fortifications and landmarks that stand as a testament to the region's strategic importance over the centuries. As I wandered through the cobblestone streets, I could almost hear the echoes of battles fought and alliances formed. Cheb is a place where history feels alive, and it's an ideal destination for anyone interested in the military past of the Czech lands.

Karlovy Vary, on the other hand, couldn't be more different, yet equally captivating. This world-famous spa town is a haven for relaxation and indulgence. As I walked along its beautiful colonnades, taking in the majestic architecture and the scent of thermal springs, I couldn't help but feel at ease. But Karlovy Vary is more than just a place to relax; it's also a town with a rich cultural calendar, particularly during the International Film Festival, which attracts film lovers from around the world. The blend of wellness, culture, and natural beauty makes this town an unforgettable destination. Then there's Mariánské Lázně, a place I found particularly special for its stunning gardens and lush landscapes. The town's charm lies in its well-preserved historic walks, lined with grand spa buildings and peaceful green spaces. It's the perfect spot for a quiet stroll, where the natural beauty and the elegant architecture create a sense of calm that's hard to find anywhere else. The parks and gardens of Mariánské Lázně are so carefully tended that it feels as though you've stepped into a living museum, a place where the past and nature are in perfect harmony.

In this chapter, I'll take you through these places, showing you the richness of Western Bohemia, a region where history, relaxation, and nature come together in the most captivating way. Whether you're a history buff, a film enthusiast, or someone looking to experience the beauty of nature, Western Bohemia has something to offer every kind of traveler. So let's dive in and explore the many facets of this fascinating region.

Military History and Scenic Views in Cheb

Cheb, a small town tucked away in the western part of the Czech Republic, was an unexpected discovery for me. Known for its deep military history and stunning views, this place captures the essence of both the past and the natural beauty of the region. As I arrived in Cheb, I could immediately sense the weight of its history. The town is like an open-air museum, with its medieval streets and towering fortifications still standing proudly, offering a rare glimpse into the Czech Republic's military heritage.

One of the first places I visited in Cheb was the Cheb Castle, which stands as a testament to the region's strategic importance during the medieval period. The castle, with its impressive walls and fortified towers, is a true architectural gem. As I walked through its halls, I could imagine the soldiers who once stood guard here, watching over the land that stretched out below. The castle has been through centuries of change, and it still holds its ground as one of the town's most iconic landmarks. I highly recommend visiting the castle's tower, where you can get a panoramic view of Cheb and the surrounding countryside. The sight from up there is absolutely breathtaking, with the rolling hills and forests creating a landscape that feels timeless.

In addition to the castle, the town of Cheb itself is filled with remnants of its military past. The town square is home to several buildings that have withstood the test of time, and wandering through these old streets feels like stepping into a different era. The Church of St. Nicholas, with its baroque architecture, is another must-see, and I found its peaceful atmosphere a perfect contrast to the more robust, historical sites. Cheb is also home to several monuments that commemorate its military history, including a memorial dedicated to soldiers who fought in both World Wars. The town's connection to the past is hard to ignore, but it's not just about the history—Cheb is also blessed with some of the most beautiful natural landscapes I've encountered. The region surrounding Cheb is perfect for outdoor activities, especially if you enjoy hiking. There are several scenic trails that wind through the nearby forests and hills, offering both peaceful solitude and sweeping views of the landscape. The Cheb region is part of the larger Slavkov Forest (Slavkovský les) area, which is known for its rich biodiversity and tranquility. I spent a day hiking in the area, and the combination of fresh air, lush forests, and panoramic vistas was unforgettable. Whether you're a history enthusiast or someone simply looking to enjoy nature, Cheb provides a perfect balance of both.

For accommodations, one of the best places to stay is the Hotel Goethe, located just a short walk from the town square. This charming, family-owned hotel offers a comfortable stay with traditional Czech hospitality. Rooms are spacious, well-furnished, and many offer scenic views of the surrounding countryside. The hotel's restaurant serves delicious Czech cuisine, and I couldn't resist trying the local specialties like roast duck with cabbage and dumplings. Prices range from $60 to $90 per night, depending on the room and season. You can contact them via phone at +420 354 441 211 or email them at info@hotelgoethecheb.cz.

If you prefer something more modern, Hotel Silesia is another great option. Situated in the center of Cheb, this hotel offers a more contemporary feel with all the amenities you'd expect. It's within walking distance of the town's historic sites, making it a convenient base for sightseeing. Rates here are around $70 to $120 per night, and the hotel has free Wi-Fi and private parking. For more details, visit their website at www.hotelsilesia.cz or contact them at +420 354 440 024. For dining, Restaurace U Tří Pštrosů is a wonderful spot to enjoy traditional Czech food.

Located just a few minutes from the castle, this restaurant offers a cozy atmosphere and an impressive menu. I highly recommend trying the beef goulash, which was rich and flavorful. Meals here range from $10 to $20, making it an affordable yet delightful experience. You can reach them at +420 354 531 616 or visit their website at www.utripstrosu.cz.

To get to Cheb, you can take a train from Prague, which takes around 2.5 to 3 hours. The train station in Cheb is well-connected, and taxis are readily available to take you directly to your accommodation or the town's key historical sites. Alternatively, you can drive to Cheb, as it's located just off the D6 motorway. The drive from Prague takes about 2.5 hours, and the town is well-signposted.

Karlovy Vary: Spa Town and Film Festival

Karlovy Vary, or Carlsbad as it's sometimes called, is a town that has a reputation for healing waters and a luxurious atmosphere that has attracted visitors for centuries. As I made my way through the cobblestone streets, I couldn't help but feel like I had stepped back in time, into an era where people traveled for wellness, relaxation, and a little indulgence. The town, nestled in the Bohemian Forest of western Czechia, is known for its spa tradition, and it's easy to see why it has earned its place as one of Europe's premier spa destinations.

I first visited Karlovy Vary as a wellness getaway and was immediately struck by how charming the town is. It's not just the therapeutic hot springs that attract visitors but also the elegant 19th-century architecture and the atmosphere of quiet sophistication. The moment you step into the main spa district, you're greeted by impressive colonnades, lavish spa buildings, and vibrant greenery. The first thing I noticed was the colonnade-lined promenade, where locals and tourists alike strolled, sipping from the mineral springs through the unique cups provided at various fountains around town. There are 12 different springs in Karlovy Vary, each with its own distinct taste and temperature, offering everything from mild to sharply salty flavors. You're encouraged to take a sip or two, but the idea is less about drinking to enjoy the taste and more about the health benefits that these naturally mineral-rich waters are said to provide.

What struck me most about Karlovy Vary is how well it balances tradition with modern luxuries. The town has been a hub of European aristocracy and royalty since the 18th century, and it retains that air of refinement. However, there is a clear emphasis on wellness and rejuvenation, with many luxurious hotels offering spa treatments that use the natural spring water. The well-known

Grandhotel Pupp, for example, is more than just a hotel. It's a spa resort where you can indulge in all kinds of treatments, from massages to specialized detox programs, all set in the most opulent surroundings. This hotel is often associated with glamour and grandeur—perhaps because of its appearances in films like The Last Holiday with Queen Latifah.

If you're not just visiting for the spa experience, Karlovy Vary is also home to one of the most prestigious film festivals in Europe, the Karlovy Vary International Film Festival. I was lucky enough to be in town during the festival and the energy around the event was absolutely electric. Film stars, directors, and film buffs from all over the world gathered to watch premieres, attend talks, and participate in one of the oldest and most prestigious film festivals in the world. The festival takes place every July, and the atmosphere is something special, with films being shown in open-air theaters and grand cinema halls. The entire town seems to come alive with screenings, parties, and lively discussions about the best films of the year. Even if you're not attending the festival, there's something exciting about being in town during this time, with the streets filled with people, movie posters, and film-themed events.

If you're planning on staying in Karlovy Vary, there are plenty of great accommodation options that will enhance your experience. For those who want to experience the grandeur of the spa tradition, the Grandhotel Pupp is a fantastic choice. Located at Mírové nám. 2, 360 01 Karlovy Vary, this historic hotel is as much about the experience as it is about the luxury. The rooms are stately and equipped with everything you'd expect, from plush bedding to high-end amenities. The hotel also has a renowned spa where you can experience treatments using the local mineral water, as well as other wellness offerings like mud wraps and thermal baths. Prices at the Grandhotel Pupp can range from $200 to $350 per night, depending on the room and season. You can contact them at +420 359 001 111 or visit their website at www.grandhotelpupp.cz for more details. For something a little more modern, the Hotel Romance Puskin, located at Stará Louka 39, 360 01 Karlovy Vary, offers a more contemporary feel with a spa and wellness center that has a range of treatments available, including massages and facials. This hotel blends modern comforts with classic elegance, and its location near the famous Hot Spring Colonnade makes it perfect for those who want to be at the center of the town's activity. Prices here range from $100 to $200 per night, and the hotel offers free Wi-Fi, a sauna, and a restaurant serving Czech cuisine. You can contact them at +420 359 220 581 or check out their website at www.romancepuskin.cz.

As for dining, Karlovy Vary has plenty of excellent restaurants, offering everything from traditional Czech food to fine dining. One place I recommend is the Restaurant U Švejka, located at

Stará Louka 22, 360 01 Karlovy Vary. This restaurant serves hearty Czech meals in a cozy, traditional setting. I tried the classic Czech dish of svíčková (marinated beef with creamy sauce and dumplings), and it was absolutely delicious. Prices here range from $10 to $20 per meal, and the atmosphere is welcoming and warm. For reservations, call +420 353 228 680.

If you're in the mood for something more upscale, head to the Restaurant Becherplatz at the Hotel Imperial, located at Libušina 1212/18, 360 01 Karlovy Vary. This Michelin-recommended restaurant offers exquisite gourmet meals and fantastic views of the town. The dishes here are as beautifully presented as they are delicious, and the service is impeccable. The price range for a meal here is from $30 to $60 per person. You can contact them at +420 353 220 191 or visit their website at www.hotelimperial.cz. Getting to Karlovy Vary is relatively simple. It's about a two-hour drive from Prague, and the journey is quite scenic. You can also take a train from Prague's main station, which takes around 3 hours and provides a comfortable, relaxing ride. Once you're in Karlovy Vary, getting around is easy on foot, as the town is compact and walkable. There are also buses and taxis available if you need to travel a bit farther out.

Whether you're coming to soak in the healing waters, attend the film festival, or simply enjoy the town's charm, Karlovy Vary is a destination that offers something for everyone. With its rich history, luxury accommodations, and a mix of relaxation and culture, it's a place that can rejuvenate both body and soul.

Gardens and Historic Walks: Exploring Mariánské Lázně

Mariánské Lázně, often known as Marienbad, is a town that perfectly captures the essence of old-world elegance and natural beauty. It's one of the Czech Republic's premier spa towns, and for good reason. I remember my first visit there—it was like stepping into a postcard. Everywhere I looked, there were lush gardens, elegant colonnades, and the soothing sounds of fountains. The air seemed fresher somehow, and every street I walked down felt like a quiet invitation to slow down, breathe, and enjoy the peace of this unique destination.

The town's history as a spa destination goes back centuries, and its healing mineral waters have attracted visitors from all over the world since the 19th century. But what really sets Mariánské Lázně apart from other spa towns is its incredible commitment to both nature and culture. The gardens and parks here are nothing short of breathtaking. You can easily spend hours wandering through them, taking in the vibrant flowers, the carefully manicured lawns, and the tranquil atmosphere that seems to define the town. I took a leisurely walk through the Dlouhá louka park and felt like I was in a fairy tale—everywhere there were tall trees, winding paths, and benches perfectly placed for you to stop and just take it all in. The gardens are an invitation to escape the noise of everyday life and embrace the calm that the town offers.

One of my favorite spots was the beautiful Singing Fountain, located near the colonnades. It's a spectacular display of water, light, and music that happens at regular intervals throughout the day. The fountain is surrounded by perfectly landscaped gardens and is a great place to relax while enjoying the view. I found a nearby bench, grabbed a cup of the local healing mineral water, and simply sat and watched the performance—it was like the world slowed down just for a moment. If you love nature and peace, Mariánské Lázně offers plenty of green spaces to unwind, all within walking distance from the main spa area.

For those who enjoy a bit of history with their strolls, Mariánské Lázně offers numerous historic walks, many of which lead you through the charming town center and up into the surrounding forests. The walks range from easy to moderate in difficulty, and each one tells a different story about the town's rich history. I took the walk that led me to the town's historic colonnades and spa houses, which are architecturally stunning and provide a glimpse into the town's heyday. The quiet streets are dotted with elegant 19th-century buildings, some of which were once frequented by famous figures like Johann Wolfgang von Goethe and Franz Kafka. Walking these streets, you can almost feel the presence of history, and I often imagined what it would have been like to visit in its prime, when royalty and aristocrats roamed the same paths. The town's spa culture is a key part of the experience, and it's impossible to visit without acknowledging the wellness aspect. If you're looking to relax and rejuvenate, there are numerous spa hotels and wellness centers offering everything from therapeutic mineral baths to luxurious massages. But even if you're not staying at a spa, you can still enjoy the therapeutic benefits of the mineral waters, which are available at various springs around the town. The most famous of these is the Ferdinand Spring, which is housed in the charmingly ornate Ferdinand Colonnade. I made sure to stop by and take a sip of the mineral water, which was said to be good for digestive health—whether or not that's true, it was a lovely experience.

As for where to stay, Mariánské Lázně offers a variety of accommodations, from historic grand hotels to modern spa resorts. If you're looking for something truly special, the Hotel Imperial is one of the top luxury hotels in the area. Located at Hlavní třída 100, 353 01 Mariánské Lázně, the

Hotel Imperial is a beautiful, classic spa hotel that combines old-world charm with modern amenities. The rooms are spacious and elegant, and the hotel offers an array of wellness treatments, from mineral baths to therapeutic massages. The hotel also boasts a fine-dining restaurant and is known for its top-notch service. Prices at Hotel Imperial range from $150 to $250 per night, depending on the room and season. You can reach them at +420 354 633 111 or visit their website at www.hotel-imperial.cz.

If you're after something more budget-friendly yet still comfortable and charming, Hotel Goethe is a great option. Located at Hlavní třída 139, 353 01 Mariánské Lázně, Hotel Goethe is a well-rated mid-range hotel that provides a cozy atmosphere and excellent service. The hotel offers a spa and wellness center with access to mineral baths, and it's just a short walk from the town center. Prices here range from $60 to $120 per night. You can contact them at +420 354 438 551 or visit their website at www.hotel-goethe.cz. When it comes to dining, Mariánské Lázně has several wonderful restaurants offering both local and international cuisine. One standout for me was Restaurant Nové Lázně, located at Anglická 210, 353 01 Mariánské Lázně, right next to the spa complex. This restaurant offers an elegant dining experience with views over the town's parks. The menu is a blend of traditional Czech dishes and European classics. I tried their veal with a rich mushroom sauce, and it was outstanding. Prices for a meal here range from $20 to $40 per person, and the service is impeccable. You can contact them at +420 354 615 555 or visit their website at www.hotel-marian.cz.

Another great option is the Restaurant Belle Époque at the Hotel Cristal Palace, located at Hlavní třída 122, 353 01 Mariánské Lázně. This is an upscale restaurant known for its exquisite menu and refined atmosphere. The cuisine is a mix of Czech and international dishes, and the wine selection is top-notch. I had a fantastic time enjoying a fine meal here, and I highly recommend it for anyone looking for a more sophisticated dining experience. Expect to spend between $30 and $50 per person for a meal. For more details, visit their website at www.cristalpalace.cz or call +420 354 689 000.

Getting to Mariánské Lázně is easy, whether you're coming from Prague or other parts of the Czech Republic. The town is about a two-hour drive from Prague, and there are regular trains and buses that connect the town to major cities like Plzeň and Karlovy Vary. The train station is located just a short distance from the town center, so you'll have no trouble reaching your hotel or the main spa areas. Once in town, the best way to get around is on foot—everything is within walking distance, and the scenic walks are part of the charm of visiting Mariánské Lázně.

CHAPTER 12

Nightlife and Entertainment

When it comes to nightlife and entertainment, the Czech Republic offers something for everyone, whether you're looking to dance the night away in a high-energy club, immerse yourself in culture at the opera, or simply enjoy the local atmosphere at a cozy pub. I first visited Prague at night and was immediately struck by how vibrant the city feels after dark—there's this undeniable energy that pulses through its streets. Whether you're in the mood for a relaxed evening or a lively night out, the options are endless.

In Prague, the nightlife is particularly diverse. The city boasts an impressive array of clubs and bars, ranging from intimate lounges tucked away in historic buildings to bustling dance floors that keep the beats going until the early hours of the morning. One night, I found myself in one of the city's underground clubs where the music, a mix of electronic and techno, seemed to sync perfectly with the energy of the crowd. But Prague isn't just about wild nights out. The city's elegant side comes alive in its cultural offerings, with the National Theatre hosting world-class opera and ballet performances that showcase the country's rich cultural heritage. The grandeur of the venue, combined with the exquisite performances, made for an unforgettable evening that balanced entertainment with sophistication. And then there are those who want something a little more interactive. From casinos where you can test your luck to unique experiences that blend technology and entertainment, the Czech Republic has plenty of opportunities for those looking for something beyond the usual bar scene.

But what really makes the Czech nightlife scene stand out are the festivals. The country has a rich tradition of yearly events, from music festivals to theatrical celebrations, and attending one of these is the perfect way to experience Czech culture in a fun and engaging way. Whether you're in town for a short time or have the luxury of planning around one of these annual events, they offer a fantastic way to connect with the local vibe.

In this chapter, I'll take you on a journey through Prague's lively night scene, introduce you to the elegance of cultural nights at the National Theatre, guide you through exciting leisure activities, and offer a glimpse into the yearly festivals that you can't miss. Whether you're here for the high-energy clubs, the refined theatre, or the unique festivals, the Czech Republic knows how to turn every night into a celebration.

Prague's Vibrant Night Scene: Clubs and Bars

Prague's nightlife is as diverse as the city itself, offering everything from laid-back cocktail bars to high-energy nightclubs. On my first visit to the city, I was immediately captivated by the after-dark scene, where the energy seems to shift from the quiet charm of the cobblestone streets to a lively and electric atmosphere that invites everyone to be part of the fun. Whether you're a seasoned night owl or just looking for a good time after a long day of sightseeing, Prague's clubs and bars have something to offer.

One of the things I loved about the Prague nightlife scene was how easy it is to find a place that matches your vibe. If you're in the mood to dance until the early morning hours, the city's clubs are top-notch. Some are housed in underground spaces with an industrial feel, while others occupy historic buildings that mix the charm of the old with the pulse of modern beats.

One night, I found myself at Roxy, one of Prague's most famous clubs, tucked in a building that dates back to the 1990s. The music—a mix of electronic, techno, and deep house—was so immersive that the crowd seemed to move in sync with the rhythms. What struck me about Roxy and many other clubs is the sense of community. People from all walks of life come together to enjoy the music and have a great time. There's no pretentiousness here; it's just about the music, the vibe, and a shared sense of celebration.

But if dancing till dawn isn't your thing, Prague's bar scene is equally exciting. Whether you prefer a traditional Czech pub, where you can enjoy a cold Pilsner and friendly conversation, or a sleek rooftop bar with stunning views over the city, the options are endless. One evening, I ventured into Hemingway Bar, an intimate cocktail lounge named after the famous author. As soon as I stepped inside, I was greeted by the soft glow of dim lighting and the enticing smell of freshly crafted cocktails. The menu features a wide range of drinks, from classic cocktails to unique concoctions created with local ingredients. Hemingway Bar has a cozy, almost speakeasy feel to it, and the knowledgeable bartenders are always ready to recommend something new based on your tastes.

For those seeking a more unique experience, Prague is full of quirky spots. I stumbled across BeerGeek, a bar dedicated to craft beer lovers. The place boasts an impressive selection of over 30 taps of Czech and international beers, and the staff is incredibly knowledgeable about the brews they serve. It's a great place for anyone who wants to dive deeper into the Czech beer culture or just enjoy a few pints with friends in a relaxed setting. Getting around the city at night is a breeze. Most of the popular nightlife areas are located within walking distance of the city center, so you can easily explore without the need for taxis or public transport. The Old Town (Staré

Město) and the neighboring New Town (Nové Město) are packed with bars and clubs, so I often found myself hopping between different spots, just following the music and lights. If you're staying a bit further out, the city's excellent metro and tram system runs late into the night, and taxis are also widely available.

If you're looking for something truly memorable, some of the larger nightclubs, like Epic, host international DJs and feature world-class light shows. It's an experience you'll want to remember, and many of these clubs are located near the Vltava River, offering breathtaking views of Prague's iconic skyline as you dance the night away.

Cultural Nights: Opera and Ballet at the National Theatre

When I first heard about the National Theatre in Prague, I didn't expect it to be such a magical part of the city's cultural fabric, but once I experienced it firsthand, I couldn't recommend it more. The National Theatre (Národní divadlo) is an iconic landmark of Czech culture and history, a place where the arts come alive in spectacular ways. Whether you're a lifelong fan of opera or ballet, or just looking for a unique cultural experience, a visit here is an unforgettable journey into the heart of Prague's artistic heritage.

Located right along the Vltava River, just a short walk from the bustling center of the city, the National Theatre's grand, neo-Renaissance building is as much a work of art as the performances staged inside. It's one of the most important cultural venues in the country, and stepping through its ornate doors, you immediately feel the weight of history. The theatre first opened its doors in 1881, and it has been the site of countless landmark performances since then. You'll notice this sense of tradition the moment you enter the main hall. The lavish interior, with its gilded balconies, grand chandeliers, and intricate frescoes, transports you to another time, making it a perfect setting for a night at the opera or ballet.

During my visit, I had the opportunity to attend a performance of the Czech National Ballet, and I was absolutely captivated. The dancers' movements were so precise and powerful, telling stories without words. And the orchestra played with such passion, weaving a rich soundscape that perfectly complemented the choreography. The National Theatre hosts a variety of performances, but I found the opera and ballet performances to be particularly stunning. The opera productions often feature renowned international singers, and the experience of hearing them live in this historic venue is something you'll want to savor. The acoustics inside the theatre are impeccable, which makes every note of the orchestra, every aria from the singers, resonate beautifully in the air. Getting to the National Theatre is relatively simple. It's located at Národní 2, 110 00 Praha 1, just a few minutes from the Charles Bridge and Old Town, making it a central and easily accessible spot for both tourists and locals. The best way to get there is by public transport, as the nearest metro station, Národní třída (Line B), is just a few steps away. Trams also run frequently in the area, and it's an easy walk from places like Wenceslas Square. If you're feeling adventurous, you can even walk along the Vltava River and enjoy the scenic views of Prague's cityscape before reaching the theatre.

For tickets, I'd highly recommend checking the official Národní divadlo website in advance, especially if you're planning to attend during the busy tourist season. I was fortunate to snag a reasonably priced seat in the upper tier, but there are a variety of ticket options ranging from more affordable balcony seats to premium options in the orchestra section. The atmosphere inside is intimate yet grand, and no matter where you sit, the experience is bound to be memorable. As for the performance itself, the National Theatre is known for offering a diverse range of shows. I loved the sense of tradition, but it's also a place that embraces modern interpretations of classic works. Some performances are more avant-garde, with contemporary takes on classic operas or ballets, while others are traditional productions that transport you back to the 18th or 19th centuries. Whatever your taste, you're likely to find something that resonates with you. The theatre also hosts various festivals throughout the year, where you can catch even more performances from Czech and international artists.

After the show, if you're looking to continue the cultural vibe, the surrounding area offers several charming cafes and restaurants where you can unwind and reflect on the evening. I found a cozy spot nearby where I could sip on a Czech pilsner and chat about the performance. It's a great way to keep the evening alive and soak in the local ambiance.

The National Theatre is not just about entertainment—it's a window into the soul of Prague, offering a chance to experience the passion, history, and artistry that define this city. It's one of those experiences where the setting, the performance, and the emotion all come together to create something that you'll carry with you long after the curtain falls. If you're in Prague, I can't stress enough how important it is to spend an evening here—it's a glimpse into the heart of Czech culture, and a memory you won't forget.

Leisure and Gaming: Casinos and Interactive Experiences

When you think about Prague, you might picture its cobbled streets, historic landmarks, or the stunning Old Town, but what about the city's leisure and gaming scene? During my visit, I quickly realized that Prague offers more than just a rich history—it also has a thriving nightlife with plenty of entertainment options for those looking to try their luck at the casinos or experience interactive gaming in a whole new way. Whether you're a seasoned player or a curious tourist, there's something for everyone.

I started my evening with a visit to one of Prague's most well-known casinos, the Casino Admiral. Located near Wenceslas Square, this place draws both locals and visitors alike with its variety of gaming options and the sleek, modern atmosphere. As I walked in, the buzz of excitement was palpable. It wasn't the dark, smoky casino environment I'd imagined; instead, the space felt bright, welcoming, and vibrant, with floor-to-ceiling windows and a contemporary design that mixed the old-world charm of Prague with modern luxury. The casino offers a wide range of table games, including blackjack, roulette, and poker, along with plenty of slot machines for those looking for a bit of fun without the pressure. There's also a sports bar, so if you're a sports fan, it's easy to keep up with your favorite games while trying your hand at the tables. What really stood out to me about Casino Admiral was the customer service. The staff was professional and friendly, explaining the games to those who were new to the casino scene. I found this to be especially helpful since I was a little unfamiliar with some of the more advanced games. Even if you're not a high roller, the experience is incredibly enjoyable and accessible.

For those who prefer a more interactive experience, I highly recommend checking out the various virtual reality (VR) gaming spots in the city. These places are becoming increasingly popular, and they offer something truly unique—an experience where you can step into completely new worlds without leaving Prague. I visited one of the city's top VR arcades, located just a short walk from the city center. The setup was impressive. Upon entering, I was handed a headset and controllers, and within seconds, I was fully immersed in a new reality. From action-packed games to more relaxed puzzle challenges, VR gaming gives you the chance to interact with your surroundings in ways that regular video games just can't replicate. It was an exhilarating experience that kept me hooked for hours. It's definitely something I'd recommend if you're looking for a new type of fun, especially if you're visiting with friends or family.

Now, when it comes to where to stay and dine if you're heading out for a gaming or leisure experience, Prague has plenty of options that cater to all tastes and budgets. I stayed at the Hotel

Intercontinental Prague, which is just a short distance from Casino Admiral and a great base for exploring the city. The hotel itself was fantastic—modern yet comfortable, with excellent service and a wonderful breakfast spread. Prices here ranged from about $120 to $180 per night, depending on the room type and season. You can easily book through their website or by calling +420 296 559 111.

As for restaurants, if you're looking to grab a bite before or after your gaming session, I'd suggest the restaurant at the casino itself for a convenient and upscale option. For something more casual, there are plenty of local spots near Wenceslas Square offering Czech specialties like goulash and schnitzels, along with international options. One of my favorites was Lokál Dlouháááá, a lively place with great local beer and hearty Czech food, just a 10-minute walk from the casino. The prices here were around $10 to $20 per meal, and the atmosphere was always buzzing, making it a perfect spot to unwind after a few rounds at the tables.

Getting to the casinos or interactive gaming spots is simple. Since Prague's public transportation system is excellent, I took the metro most of the time. The Casino Admiral is easily accessible from the Můstek metro station (Lines A and B), and if you're heading to the VR arcades, many are also located near public transit hubs, making it a breeze to hop on a tram or metro. Taxis are available too, but I found that public transport is often quicker and cheaper, especially during peak times.

Yearly Festivals: An Overview

Visiting the Czech Republic is an absolute treat for anyone who loves festivals and celebrations. Over the course of the year, this country comes alive with a variety of events, from music and film festivals to traditional folk celebrations and modern art exhibits. I was fortunate enough to experience several of them during my time there, and they truly offer a window into the heart of Czech culture. Each festival brings its own special energy, and as a traveler, it's a fantastic way to get a deeper sense of the local vibe.

One of the biggest highlights for me was attending the Prague Spring International Music Festival, which kicks off every May. It's a world-class event that attracts top-notch orchestras and soloists from around the globe. I remember sitting in the beautiful Rudolfinum concert hall, soaking in the incredible acoustics as a renowned orchestra performed symphonies that left the audience in awe. The atmosphere was electric, with locals and visitors alike dressed in their finest, making the whole experience feel like a grand celebration of classical music. But it's not just about the performances themselves. The entire city seems to hum with excitement during the festival, and you'll find outdoor performances, pop-up music events, and street musicians all adding to the festive ambiance. The Prague Spring festival is definitely something I would recommend if you're into classical music or just want to witness a cultural experience that resonates with both locals and international visitors.

Another festival that truly left an impression on me was the Karlovy Vary International Film Festival. As a lover of cinema, I couldn't miss this one. This festival, held every July in the picturesque spa town of Karlovy Vary, is one of the most important film events in Central Europe. The charming town, with its elegant spa buildings and lush greenery, serves as the perfect backdrop for what's often referred to as the Czech version of Cannes. I remember walking along the streets lined with celebrities, filmmakers, and eager film enthusiasts, all coming together to celebrate the magic of cinema. The festival showcases a diverse selection of films from around the world, and it's an incredible opportunity to see a variety of indie, art-house, and international films that you might not get the chance to see elsewhere. And, of course, there are the glamorous evening galas and the chance to rub elbows with directors, actors, and producers. Even if you're not a film buff, the whole experience of being in a town buzzing with creative energy and excitement is contagious.

But festivals aren't just about the arts. In the Czech Republic, traditional events play an important role in maintaining the cultural fabric of the country. I stumbled upon one of these during my trip to Brno, where I experienced the Brno Christmas Market. While it's held in December, the spirit of the market lasts throughout the holiday season. This festival is one of the oldest and largest in the country, and it's hard not to be enchanted by the sight of beautifully decorated wooden stalls selling handcrafted gifts, local treats, and hot drinks. The smell of mulled wine and roasted chestnuts filled the air, and there was a distinct sense of warmth despite the chilly winter temperatures. Whether you're sipping a hot chocolate, trying local pastries like trdelník (a sweet, doughy treat), or simply soaking in the festive atmosphere, this Christmas market is a must-visit if you're in Brno during the winter months.

Czech festivals also celebrate the country's folk traditions. The Slovácko Festival, held every August in the town of Uherské Hradiště, is one that stands out. I was lucky enough to attend and was amazed by the vibrant costumes, lively dances, and beautiful music that filled the streets. The festival is a celebration of Czech folk traditions, with local bands playing folk tunes, traditional dancers performing intricate steps, and vendors offering handmade crafts. The Slovácko Festival is the perfect place to immerse yourself in the Czech cultural experience, where every step you take feels like a journey back in time. The festival brings together people from all over the country, creating an atmosphere of unity and pride in Czech heritage. It was one of the most fun, high-energy festivals I've attended and gave me a deeper appreciation for the local traditions.

One thing I noticed throughout all the festivals I attended is how much they value family participation. It's not unusual to see parents bringing their children along to watch a performance or join in on a dance. For me, this made the whole experience feel much more inclusive and welcoming. The festivals in the Czech Republic offer an opportunity not just for tourists, but also for locals, to come together and celebrate the things that make their culture so unique. If you plan on visiting during festival season, it's good to book accommodations in advance. Many of the festivals, especially in Prague and Karlovy Vary, attract large crowds, so hotels fill up quickly.

I found that during the Prague Spring Music Festival and Karlovy Vary International Film Festival, prices for hotels can range from $100 to $250 per night depending on location and type of accommodation. Booking early can save you the hassle of finding last-minute rooms. As for getting around during festivals, public transport in Prague and other cities is efficient, and you can easily take a tram, bus, or metro to get to most festival venues. If you're attending a festival in a smaller town, trains and buses are also convenient options, and they're often an enjoyable part of the experience as they allow you to see more of the Czech countryside.

CHAPTER 13

Activities for Different Travelers

When it comes to traveling in the Czech Republic, there's no shortage of activities that cater to a wide range of interests and types of travelers.

Whether you're a solo adventurer seeking solitude and new experiences, a couple looking for a romantic getaway, a family with kids eager for fun and learning, a senior traveler seeking comfort and easy access, or a group in need of coordinated adventures, the Czech Republic has something to offer. I've had the chance to experience this first-hand, and I can tell you that the country does an incredible job of catering to all kinds of travelers. For solo travelers like myself, the country offers an array of custom tours, from exploring the vibrant streets of Prague to hiking through the scenic Bohemian and Moravian landscapes. I was able to tailor my own experiences, diving into everything from history tours to food walks, each designed to allow me to discover the Czech Republic at my own pace and on my own terms. Whether you're seeking deep cultural exploration or the quietude of nature, there's no shortage of solo-friendly activities.

Couples will find plenty to love, too. The Czech Republic is an incredibly romantic destination. I remember strolling hand-in-hand through the charming streets of Český Krumlov, stopping by cozy cafés and enjoying peaceful moments along the Vltava River. Romantic retreats are not hard to find here, whether it's a candlelit dinner in an intimate restaurant, a stay at a luxurious spa hotel, or a sunset boat ride. It's easy to see why so many couples flock to this beautiful country to celebrate anniversaries or simply get away from the hustle and bustle of daily life. Families, especially those traveling with children, will appreciate the variety of family-friendly attractions and activities. From the magical world of Prague's zoo and gardens to interactive museums and castles that capture the imagination, there's something for every young explorer. I took a trip to the Bohemian Paradise with my cousins and was blown away by how accessible and engaging it was for kids. The natural rock formations and the castles were like something straight out of a fairy tale, and there were plenty of educational elements that kept them both entertained and learning.

For seniors, the Czech Republic offers accessible tourism that makes traveling comfortable without sacrificing any of the charm. The country has excellent transport options, from easily navigable public transport systems to accessible paths in many of the historic sites. I remember visiting the beautiful spa town of Karlovy Vary and feeling at ease with all the amenities that make it easy for seniors to enjoy a slow-paced but enriching experience. The focus on comfort and accessibility truly stands out, allowing for an enjoyable trip without the stress. And when it comes to groups, the Czech Republic offers some truly fantastic group tour options. I took part in a small group walking tour through Prague and it was an absolute blast. There's something special about exploring the city with others, sharing stories, and learning together from a knowledgeable guide. Whether it's a corporate retreat or a group of friends, there's no shortage of activities that bring people together for a shared experience.

In this chapter, I'll take you through some of the best activities for each of these traveler types, offering ideas, recommendations, and tips on how to make the most of your time in the Czech Republic. From solo expeditions to family excursions, the country provides endless opportunities to explore, relax, and connect. You'll soon see how this destination can be a perfect fit for any type of traveler, with something for everyone no matter who you are or what your interests may be.

Solo Travelers: Custom Tours and Activities

When I first traveled to the Czech Republic as a solo adventurer, I was looking for experiences that would give me the freedom to explore at my own pace while still offering unique, local insights. I quickly realized that one of the best ways to experience the country is through custom tours and activities. The Czech Republic is incredibly rich in history, culture, and natural beauty, and there's something special about crafting an experience that aligns with your personal interests and travel style. What I found, and what I think any solo traveler will love, is that there are numerous custom tours and activities tailored just for people like us—those who want to discover more than just the typical tourist attractions.

One of the highlights of my trip was a custom walking tour of Prague, which I arranged through a local company called Prague Private Tours. They specialize in crafting personalized walking tours based on your interests, whether you're into history, architecture, local cuisine, or hidden gems. I remember chatting with the guide before the tour, discussing what I wanted to see—like a mix of historic sites and off-the-beaten-path locations. The flexibility of the tour meant I could take my time in places that intrigued me, without feeling rushed. The guides were not only knowledgeable but also passionate about sharing insider tips and stories that you wouldn't find in a guidebook. The experience cost me around $70-$100 USD for a 3-4 hour private tour, but it was totally worth it for the personalized experience. They're based in Prague, and getting there is easy since they can meet you at your hotel or at a convenient landmark in the city center. You can book directly through their website: [pragueprivatetours.com](https://www.praguepriv atetours.com), or reach them by email at info@pragueprivatetours.com.

For those interested in something a bit more adventurous, Bohemian Adventures offers customizable hiking and biking tours through the scenic Bohemian countryside. I took a half-day hiking trip through the lush forests of the Bohemian Paradise (a UNESCO-protected natural site) and was amazed by how secluded and peaceful it felt. The guide tailored the route based on my level of fitness, and we spent hours winding through rock formations, caves, and small, picturesque villages. This was exactly the kind of custom experience that let me explore the natural beauty of the country at my own pace. Their rates are generally in the $100-$150 USD range for a half-day trip, and they can be contacted at info@bohemianadventures.com. Their website is (https://www.bohemianadventures.com), and their tours are based in Prague, but they will arrange transportation to wherever your adventure starts.

Another great solo experience I stumbled upon was a Czech Beer Tasting Tour, which I booked with Czech Beer Tours. This tour was a perfect way to dive deep into the country's world-renowned beer culture. As a solo traveler, I was looking for a way to enjoy the local flavors while learning something new. This 3-hour guided beer tour took me through several microbreweries and pubs in Prague, where I tasted a variety of Czech beers and learned about the brewing process and the country's beer history. The tour was totally customizable based on the types of beer I preferred, and the guide made sure to explain each beer's unique characteristics, from pale lagers to dark stouts. At around $60 USD, the tour was a great value, and it was a fantastic way to meet fellow travelers and chat with locals in a relaxed setting. You can book directly on their website at (https://www.czechbeertours.com), or email them at info@czechbeertours.com.

If you're someone who prefers a bit of luxury, Czech Spa Tours offers tailored wellness experiences in places like Karlovy Vary and Mariánské Lázně, where you can unwind and recharge in the country's world-famous thermal spas. I booked a full-day spa tour with a private driver and guide, where I had the chance to experience both the healing waters and a traditional spa treatment. The guide was wonderful, giving me historical background on the spas while ensuring I got the most out of my visit. This kind of tour costs around $150-$200 USD for a full day, but for solo travelers looking to indulge in relaxation, it's a perfect option. The website for booking is (https://www.czechspatours.com), and they can be reached at info@czechspatours.com.

Couples: Romantic Retreats and Activities

When my partner and I first decided to visit the Czech Republic, we were looking for a romantic getaway that offered a balance of both adventure and relaxation. Little did we know, this beautiful country had everything we could have dreamed of—charming cities, stunning landscapes, and countless ways to enjoy a peaceful, intimate retreat together. From exploring medieval castles to unwinding in luxurious spas, the Czech Republic offers a range of activities that make it an ideal destination for couples seeking romance and connection.

One of our favorite experiences was a scenic boat cruise along the Vltava River in Prague. As we drifted past the iconic Charles Bridge, with the sun setting behind Prague Castle, it felt like we had stepped into a postcard. The boat was small and intimate, offering a perfect vantage point to admire the city's beautiful architecture. The cruise also included a delicious three-course dinner, which was the cherry on top of an already magical evening. We booked the cruise through Prague Boats, and the experience cost us around $50 per person, including dinner. We set off from the pier at Dvořákovo nábřeží, just a short walk from the city center. The company's website, (https://www.prague-boats.cz), is easy to navigate, and booking ahead is a great idea, especially during peak tourist season.

For couples who enjoy a bit of history mixed with romance, there are plenty of opportunities to explore the Czech Republic's castles and palaces. One of the most unforgettable experiences we had was visiting Karlštejn Castle, a majestic Gothic castle just a short drive from Prague. The castle sits atop a hill, surrounded by lush forests, and the views from the top are simply breathtaking. We took a guided tour that provided fascinating insight into the castle's history, but what really made it special was the intimate setting and peaceful atmosphere. Afterward, we enjoyed a quiet lunch at a local café, surrounded by the charm of the village. The cost for entry to the castle was about $15 per person, and guided tours were available for an additional $10 per person. We rented a car to get there, but there are also public transport options from Prague if you prefer not to drive.

Of course, no romantic trip is complete without a bit of pampering. One of the most romantic experiences we had was a day at the luxurious Spa Hotel Imperial in Karlovy Vary, a famous spa town about two hours from Prague. The hotel's spa offers a range of rejuvenating treatments, including couples' massages, thermal baths, and mud wraps. We spent the day relaxing in the thermal pools, enjoying the peaceful atmosphere of the spa, and then had a candlelit dinner at the hotel's elegant restaurant. The cost for a day at the spa varied depending on the treatments you choose, but a couples' massage and access to the thermal pools was around $150 for both of us. Getting to Karlovy Vary from Prague is easy with a direct bus ride or by train, and it's definitely worth the journey for a truly indulgent experience.

For couples who want to experience the natural beauty of the Czech Republic together, I highly recommend a visit to the Bohemian Switzerland National Park, located near the German border. We took a guided hiking tour through the park, which is known for its stunning sandstone rock formations and lush green forests. The hike was not only a beautiful experience, but it also offered plenty of opportunities to pause, take in the views, and enjoy the quiet serenity of nature. The tour lasted about 5 hours, and the cost was around $70 per person. It was an unforgettable day, and we felt like we had the whole park to ourselves, surrounded by nature's beauty. You can reach the park easily from Prague via a 2.5-hour train ride, and there are also private transport options available if you prefer a more direct route.

For a more relaxed, low-key romantic experience, consider spending a few hours wandering around the charming town of Český Krumlov. This UNESCO World Heritage site feels like something out of a fairy tale, with its cobblestone streets, medieval town square, and the impressive Český Krumlov Castle overlooking the Vltava River.

We spent the day strolling hand-in-hand, visiting art galleries, and enjoying a cozy lunch at one of the town's charming cafés. The town's relaxed pace made it a perfect destination for couples seeking a more intimate, slow-paced experience. You can easily reach Český Krumlov from Prague by bus or train, and the journey takes about 3 hours.

Family Ventures: Attractions Suited for Children

When I visited the Czech Republic with my family, I quickly realized that this country isn't just for history buffs or party-goers—it's also an ideal destination for families with children. From castles to zoos and interactive museums, the Czech Republic is filled with attractions that will keep young ones engaged and entertained while providing fun for the whole family. We discovered so many hidden gems that I'd love to share with other families planning their trip.

One of the first stops on our family adventure was the Prague Zoo, located in the Troja district, just a short bus ride from the city center. I have to say, it's one of the best zoos I've ever visited. Spread out over a large area, the zoo is home to thousands of animals, including everything from elephants and gorillas to endangered species like the Amur tiger. What made this zoo stand out was how thoughtfully it's designed—there are spacious habitats for the animals, and plenty of shaded areas and rest stops for families. My kids loved the petting zoo, where they got to interact with goats and sheep, and the pavilions housing exotic creatures like the Komodo dragon. The zoo is also educational, with fun, hands-on exhibits for kids that teach them about wildlife conservation. Tickets are affordable, usually around $10 for adults and $5 for children, and you can easily get there by taking bus number 112 from the Nádraží Holešovice metro station.

Another unforgettable stop for our family was the National Technical Museum in Prague. This place was a huge hit with my kids, who couldn't stop exploring all the interactive exhibits. Located in a beautifully restored building in the Letná district, the museum features exhibits on everything from aviation to astronomy and even vintage cars. The highlight for us was the section dedicated to trains, where kids could climb into the driver's cabin of old steam engines. There are plenty of hands-on activities, so it's not just a place to look—it's a place to touch, learn, and experience. Tickets are around $10 for adults and $5 for kids. The museum is easily accessible by tram or bus, and it's just a short ride from the city center. It's a perfect way to spend a few hours, especially on a rainy day.

If you have little ones who are still in the "hands-on, touch-everything" phase, I highly recommend visiting the Prague Planetarium. It's located near the Stromovka park, and it's an excellent way to introduce children to the wonders of the universe. Inside, you'll find interactive exhibits that let kids play with models of planets and stars, as well as a space for stargazing. The planetarium also offers educational shows, which can be a fun and immersive experience for the whole family. We attended a show that took us on a virtual tour of the night sky, and my children were absolutely captivated. Tickets here are about $6 for children and $12 for adults, and it's easy to get there via tram or metro. For a more nature-focused adventure, the Bohemian Paradise (Český ráj) National Park, located about an hour and a half outside of Prague, is a wonderful family destination. This UNESCO Global Geopark is known for its dramatic sandstone rock formations, forests, and castles. My family spent a day hiking through the park, and it was a fantastic mix of outdoor fun and history. The kids loved exploring the rock formations and climbing up to the ruins of Trosky Castle. The park is family-friendly, with trails that are not too challenging for younger hikers. We made a day of it, packing a picnic and enjoying the fresh air. The area is easily accessible by car from Prague, or you can take a train to Turnov, where you can pick up a bus to the park. Entrance to the park is free, though some of the castles or lookout points may have small entry fees of around $5 to $10.

One experience that truly stood out was our visit to the DinoPark in Prague, which is a must-see for any dinosaur lover. Located at the Prague Zoo, this park is home to life-sized dinosaur models that move and make noises, providing a thrilling experience for younger children. The park also has a 3D cinema, where we watched an animated film about dinosaurs. It's a bit of a theme park experience, but it's educational as well, with plenty of information about each species of dinosaur. The kids were in awe the entire time, and it was one of those moments where I saw their imaginations truly come to life. Entrance is about $10 for adults and $7 for children. You can buy tickets at the entrance or as part of a combined ticket with the zoo.

If your family enjoys amusement parks, there's also the Aquapalace Praha, one of the largest water parks in Central Europe. Located just outside of Prague, it's a short trip by car or public transportation, and it's a great way to spend an entire day. The water park features everything from lazy rivers and wave pools to thrilling water slides. It's perfect for families with kids of all ages, and there's even a wellness area for parents to relax while the kids have fun. The cost is around $20 per adult and $15 per child for a full-day pass, and there are discounts for groups or longer visits.

Lastly, for families who want to experience something a little different, I highly recommend a trip to the Český Krumlov Castle. This fairy-tale-like castle is a great place for families, with plenty of spaces to explore, including the castle's gardens, the baroque theater, and even the castle's tower. We took a guided tour that was fun and informative for the kids, and they especially loved learning about the castle's history and legends. The castle is located in the charming town of Český Krumlov, which is about a 3-hour drive or a 4-hour train ride from Prague. Entry to the castle is around $10 to $15, depending on the tour.

Seniors: Accessible Tourism and Comfort Travel

When my parents visited the Czech Republic, they were initially concerned about whether the country would be easy for them to explore given their need for comfort and accessibility. What I found during our trip, however, was a surprisingly accommodating environment for seniors, with plenty of options for relaxation, sightseeing, and convenience. Whether you're seeking accessible transport, barrier-free attractions, or simply a slower pace, the Czech Republic has much to offer.

One of the first things I noticed when navigating the city with my parents was the accessibility of public transportation, especially in Prague. The city has made significant strides in creating barrier-free access, particularly in the metro system. For example, many stations now feature elevators, wide entryways, and ramps to ensure ease of movement. If you're traveling by tram or bus, it's also worth noting that these are typically equipped with low floors and easy-to-use ramps. The best part is that seniors often receive discounts for public transport, which is both a great financial benefit and a sign of how the city is working to make travel easier for older visitors. The tram system, which runs throughout Prague, is particularly convenient for getting around the city without needing to walk too far or deal with stairs.

For seniors seeking a more leisurely pace, I highly recommend a visit to the Prague Castle. Although the castle is perched on a hill, there are accessible routes available, including a car service that takes visitors directly to the top. Once there, the areas around the castle are very accessible, with wide paths, benches, and plenty of shady spots to rest. Inside the castle complex, many of the exhibits and spaces are wheelchair-friendly, and the staff is incredibly helpful with providing assistance when needed. The castle is located in the Hradčany district, and you can easily get there from the city center by tram or taxi. For a more comfortable experience, taking a guided tour can also help minimize walking and ensure a relaxed pace.

Another great option for seniors is a cruise along the Vltava River in Prague. The river cruises are a relaxing way to take in the city's beautiful architecture without exerting too much effort. Many of these boats are wheelchair accessible, and they offer covered, comfortable seating where you can enjoy the scenery in style. I took a lunch cruise with my parents, and we enjoyed a lovely three-hour journey past Prague's most famous landmarks, such as the Charles Bridge and the National Theatre. It was a stress-free experience with an audio guide that provided fascinating details about the city's history, and the staff was attentive and accommodating. The cruises depart from several spots along the river, and getting there is easy by walking or using public transport. Prices vary but generally range from $25 to $50 per person depending on the cruise type and duration. For those who are looking to venture out of Prague, the town of Český Krumlov is a great destination for seniors seeking comfort and beauty. This UNESCO-listed town is famous for its picturesque medieval streets, charming old town, and impressive castle. While the streets can be cobblestone and uneven in some places, the town is compact and easy to navigate. The castle is fully accessible, with an elevator to take you to the higher floors, offering stunning views of the town and the Vltava River. To get to Český Krumlov, it's best to take a train from Prague, which takes about 2.5 hours, and then a short walk or taxi ride from the station to the town center.

For a more rejuvenating experience, the Czech Republic is also home to several world-class spa towns, with Karlovy Vary being the most famous. This elegant town, known for its healing thermal waters, offers the perfect retreat for seniors looking to relax and pamper themselves. My parents absolutely loved the calming atmosphere, and we spent several days enjoying the therapeutic benefits of the mineral springs. Many hotels and spas in Karlovy Vary cater specifically to seniors, with easy access to the spring waters, massage treatments, and wellness therapies. The town is very senior-friendly, with plenty of accessible paths and seating areas. It's also easy to reach by train from Prague, which takes about 2.5 hours. Once there, you'll find a range of hotels that offer packages for seniors, which may include treatments and guided tours of the town's famous hot springs.

If you're looking for a comfortable experience while exploring nature, the Czech Republic's national parks also offer accessible hiking routes. The Bohemian Switzerland National Park, located near the German border, is a favorite among nature lovers. The park is home to stunning sandstone formations, cliffs, and valleys, and some of the hiking trails are designed for accessibility, including wheelchair-friendly paths. During our trip to the park, we found several easy, level trails that offered breathtaking views without being physically demanding. It's a great way to enjoy nature at a relaxed pace. The park is about 2 hours from Prague by car, and there are bus services that connect with major towns like Děčín, where you can easily reach the park.

For those who prefer an indoor cultural experience, the National Museum in Prague is another excellent option. The museum has been fully renovated and is designed with accessibility in mind, featuring elevators, ramps, and wide doorways. The exhibitions are rich with history, and the museum's staff is attentive to the needs of senior visitors, offering assistance and guiding them to the most accessible areas. The museum is centrally located, right on Wenceslas Square, and is easily reached by public transport. In terms of accommodations, the Czech Republic offers many senior-friendly hotels with accessible rooms and features like elevators, ramps, and on-site dining options. Many of the higher-end hotels in Prague, such as the Hotel Paris Prague or the Four Seasons, cater specifically to guests with accessibility needs. These hotels often provide amenities like wheelchair rentals, concierge services to assist with sightseeing arrangements, and even accessible private transfers. Additionally, many hotels offer special rates for seniors, making it more affordable to enjoy a luxurious and comfortable stay.

Groups: Activities Tour

When I traveled with a group of friends to the Czech Republic, we quickly realized that this country offers a wealth of group-oriented activities, making it an ideal destination for travelers looking to experience its rich culture, history, and natural beauty together. The key to enjoying group travel in the Czech Republic is finding the right tours and activities that offer a seamless blend of adventure, relaxation, and shared experience. Whether you're interested in exploring the vibrant streets of Prague, discovering medieval towns, or venturing into the countryside, there are numerous options for groups that want to make the most of their time in this stunning country.

One of the most popular group activities in Prague is a guided walking tour of the city's historic Old Town. These tours usually take you through the winding streets of the Old Town Square, past the astronomical clock, and to landmarks like the

Charles Bridge and the iconic Prague Castle. I did one of these tours with a group of 12, and it was the perfect way to discover Prague's history without feeling rushed. The guide was incredibly knowledgeable, sharing fascinating stories and legends about the city's past. The best part about group tours like this is that they allow for interaction with the guide, making the experience feel more personal. Prices for a half-day walking tour range from $30 to $50 per person, depending on the size of the group and whether it's a private or public tour. These tours typically include transportation by foot, so they are easy to access from anywhere in the city, with meeting points often located near major attractions like Wenceslas Square or the Old Town Square.

For those looking to explore beyond the city, there are several group tour options to visit places like Český Krumlov, a charming town known for its medieval architecture and stunning castle. My group opted for a full-day tour to Český Krumlov, which included a guided walk through the town and a visit to the famous castle. The tour also included a relaxing riverboat ride on the Vltava River, offering a scenic way to appreciate the town's beauty from the water. These day trips typically cost between $60 to $80 per person, and include transportation by bus or minivan, which makes it convenient for larger groups to travel together. Tours usually depart from Prague early in the morning and return by late afternoon, giving you enough time to explore the town without feeling rushed. To book, you can find reputable tour operators like Prague Tours Direct (www.praguetoursdirect.com), which offers various day trips to Český Krumlov, and they can be reached at +420 777 129 001 or info@praguetoursdirect.com.

For a more immersive experience, you might want to consider a group wine-tasting tour in the Moravia region, which is renowned for its excellent wines. Our group of ten enjoyed a visit to one of the family-run vineyards in the South Moravia area, where we sampled a variety of local wines and learned about the wine-making process. These tours often include a visit to the vineyard, wine cellars, and a delicious meal paired with local wines. We were able to spend the afternoon relaxing in the vineyard's beautiful surroundings, and the experience was both educational and enjoyable. Prices for these tours generally range from $50 to $75 per person, depending on the number of tastings and meals included. To get to the region from Prague, it takes about 2.5 hours by car or train, and you can book group tours with companies like Moravia Wine Tours (www.moraviawinetours.com), which offers custom itineraries and can be contacted at info@moraviawinetours.com or +420 724 550 646.

If your group is looking for something a bit more adventurous, the Czech Republic offers plenty of outdoor activities such as hiking, cycling, and even hot air ballooning. For example, we did a group cycling tour through the lush forests of Bohemian Switzerland National Park, located near the German border. The tour took us through some of the most breathtaking landscapes in the country, and it was well-suited for all fitness levels, as there were plenty of stops to rest and admire the scenery. Our guide made sure everyone in the group was comfortable and kept a relaxed pace throughout the day.

A guided cycling tour through Bohemian Switzerland usually costs between $40 and $70 per person, depending on the length of the tour and the type of bike provided. The park is about a two-hour drive from Prague, and can be reached by car or by a direct train to the nearby town of Děčín. One company that offers these types of outdoor tours is Outdoor Czech Tours (www.outdoorczech.com), which specializes in active experiences in the Czech countryside. You can contact them at info@outdoorczech.com or call +420 602 343 181. For those who are more interested in the cultural side of things, I would recommend booking a group cooking class in Prague. During our trip, we joined a group cooking class where we learned how to make traditional Czech dishes like svíčková (a creamy beef dish) and trdelník (a sweet pastry). It was a fantastic way to bond with my fellow travelers, and the class was led by a friendly local chef who shared both recipes and stories about Czech culinary traditions. Cooking classes usually cost between $50 and $80 per person, and they often include a meal at the end where you get to enjoy your creations.

Many of these classes are located near the city center, easily accessible by public transport. One of the top providers is Czech Cooking Class (www.czechcookingclass.com), which offers private and group cooking sessions. You can reach them at info@czechcookingclass.com or call +420 731 283 444.

CHAPTER 14

Itineraries

When I first set foot in the Czech Republic, I quickly realized just how much this beautiful country has to offer. From the cobbled streets of Prague to the quaint charm of Český Krumlov, there's something captivating around every corner. But one of the best ways to truly experience all that the Czech Republic has to offer is by organizing your time wisely. Whether you're visiting for a short weekend getaway or planning a longer, more immersive journey, it's all about striking the right balance between exploring the bustling cities, relaxing in picturesque towns, and enjoying the countryside's serene landscapes. In this chapter, I'll share with you some practical and carefully thought-out itineraries that I personally found to be an excellent way to experience the country.

We'll start with day trips—perfect for those staying in Prague and wanting to explore some of the nearby gems that are just a short journey away. I can tell you, these excursions are a fantastic way to get out of the city and discover medieval towns, natural wonders, and hidden corners that are often overlooked by tourists. Then, we'll dive into structured 3-day plans for a brief visit. These will help you make the most out of a short stay while covering key attractions. If you have a bit more time, I'll walk you through a detailed 7-day itinerary, giving you ample time to take in both the major cities and charming countryside. And for those lucky enough to be staying for two weeks, I'll offer an extensive 2-week guide that covers everything from the capital to the farthest reaches of the country, ensuring you get a well-rounded experience.

Throughout this chapter, I'll include not only the destinations and highlights but also practical advice on how to move around, where to stay, and how to plan your days so you don't feel rushed. It's all about creating an itinerary that suits your pace and interests, whether that means slowing down to savor every moment or pushing through to see it all. Whether you're a first-time visitor or a seasoned traveler, these itineraries are designed to help you get the most out of your Czech Republic adventure. So, let's dive in, and I'll guide you through the perfect plans for your Czech journey.

Organizing Day Trips: From Prague to Nearby Gems

When you're based in Prague, you'll quickly realize that the city itself offers so much to explore, but there's also a world of fantastic day trips waiting just beyond its borders. One of the best parts of staying in Prague is its perfect location for accessing nearby towns, villages, and natural wonders that will make you feel like you've entered a completely different world—often with just a short train or bus ride away. During my travels, I quickly learned that organizing these day trips isn't as difficult as it may seem. In fact, with a bit of planning, you can pack in so much more without feeling rushed.

If you only have a limited amount of time and want to experience something beyond Prague's historic charm, I recommend starting with a visit to Český Krumlov. It's one of the most picturesque towns I've seen in Europe, with its colorful buildings hugging the Vltava River, a stunning medieval castle, and winding alleyways that seem to whisper stories of old. The best part? It's only about two and a half hours from Prague by bus, and you'll get a chance to see a completely different side of the country. I remember stepping off the bus and immediately feeling like I had walked into a fairytale. The town's cobbled streets are lined with artisan shops, cozy cafés, and plenty of history, making it ideal for a full day of exploration. You can take a guided tour to dive deep into its past or simply wander around soaking in the beauty.

Another gem I absolutely loved was Kutná Hora, just an hour away by train. This small town packs a lot of punch with its UNESCO-listed Bone Church—Sedlec Ossuary—and the stunning St. Barbara's Church. Both sites are visually striking and filled with stories that will fascinate anyone interested in history or the eerie side of things. I visited in the morning, and after touring the Bone Church, I took a relaxed walk through the town's medieval square. There's something peaceful about exploring Kutná Hora, and I felt like I could have stayed for hours, just enjoying the atmosphere.

If you're into nature and the outdoors, a day trip to Karlovy Vary might be more your style. About two hours from Prague, this spa town offers beautiful scenery with its famous hot springs and lush surrounding hills. As I walked along the colonnades and tried the various mineral waters from the town's different springs, I couldn't help but relax and enjoy the slow pace of life. The town also offers several hiking trails that take you up into the hills, where you'll be rewarded with panoramic views of the surrounding forest and town below.

For those who enjoy exploring caves, the Koněprusy Caves, just about an hour from Prague by car, are a must-see. These are the largest cave system in Bohemia, and when I visited, I was absolutely awestruck by the beautiful stalactites and stalagmites, which seemed to form intricate shapes. You can take a guided tour of the caves, and trust me, it's worth it to hear the fascinating stories about their discovery and the way the formations have developed over centuries.

One of the most convenient ways to get to these spots is by taking a train, as Czech trains are affordable, efficient, and easy to navigate. There are also several private bus companies that run day trips from Prague to many of these destinations, offering a comfortable ride and often a tour guide who will enrich your experience with local knowledge. If you prefer a bit more flexibility, renting a car is another option that allows you to set your own pace and stop at smaller villages or hidden gems along the way. In general, day trips are easy to organize and don't require extensive planning, especially since many of these destinations are well connected to Prague via public transport.

Brief Visits: Structured 3-Day Plans

When I first visited the Czech Republic, I had just a few days to experience as much as possible. It seemed like a challenge at first, but as I quickly learned, it's entirely doable to see a lot in a short amount of time—especially if you plan your days thoughtfully. If you're only in the country for three days, there's a way to balance a bit of everything: iconic sights, culture, and a touch of nature, all while keeping the pace manageable. Having experienced a few three-day trips myself, I've come to realize that the key to enjoying your time in the Czech Republic lies in focusing on a few key spots that encapsulate the country's charm without feeling rushed.

Day one, I'd suggest diving straight into Prague, as the city is the beating heart of the Czech Republic and really gives you a taste of its history, culture, and vibe. Start your day early, visiting Prague Castle, which towers over the city. As you wander through the castle grounds, you'll get a sense of Prague's medieval past. The Gothic-style St. Vitus Cathedral within the complex is truly breathtaking and offers panoramic views of the city. After soaking in the history, walk down the hill to the Vltava River and cross the Charles Bridge, where the statues of saints line the bridge and give the whole area a surreal, almost otherworldly feel. By now, you'll be ready for lunch in the Old Town, and I highly recommend finding a spot in one of the little squares where you can people-watch while enjoying Czech classics like svíčková (beef in creamy sauce) or goulash. After lunch, take a stroll through Prague's Old Town Square, where you'll find the Astronomical Clock and plenty of historical buildings. A quick stop at the Jewish Quarter, or Josefov, will give you a glimpse into another side of the city with its centuries-old synagogues and poignant museums. Finish your first day with a casual walk along the Vltava riverbank, perhaps even catching a sunset by the water.

On day two, venture out of Prague to explore a nearby destination, and for a day trip, nothing quite beats Český Krumlov. A two-and-a-half-hour bus ride from Prague, this charming town feels like something straight out of a fairytale, with its winding streets, medieval buildings, and the dramatic Krumlov Castle perched above the Vltava River. When I visited, I found myself wandering the narrow cobbled streets, just soaking in the scenery. The castle is an essential stop here, and it's impressive not only because of its size and history but also for its beautiful Baroque theatre and gardens.

After visiting the castle, I recommend strolling along the river, where you can rent a kayak or take a boat trip, offering an entirely different perspective of the town. Don't forget to check out some of the local artisan shops, where you can pick up handcrafted souvenirs to remember your time in this magical place. You'll also want to grab lunch at one of the local taverns, enjoying a hearty meal in a cozy, rustic setting. By the end of the day, you'll have truly immersed yourself in the tranquil atmosphere of Český Krumlov, with its rich history and laid-back charm.

On your third day, if you're craving a little nature, head toward the Bohemian Switzerland National Park, a little over an hour away from Prague by train and bus. The park is famous for its dramatic sandstone rock formations, deep valleys, and dense forests, which look like they've been pulled straight from a fantasy novel. I spent the day hiking the easy-to-follow trails that lead to some of the park's most famous spots, including the Pravčická Brána, the largest natural sandstone arch in Europe. It's a bit of a hike to get there, but the views from the top are so worth it. If hiking isn't your thing, there are also boat trips you can take along the Kamenice River through the gorge, offering a more relaxed way to see the stunning scenery. Whether you decide to hike or enjoy a peaceful boat ride, the beauty of Bohemian

Switzerland is sure to leave a lasting impression. After a day in nature, head back to Prague in the evening, where you can enjoy a final dinner in the city, perhaps in one of the traditional beer halls that are so popular in the Czech Republic.

By the time your three days are up, you'll have experienced a well-rounded glimpse of the Czech Republic—its vibrant capital, fairytale towns, and unspoiled natural beauty. Even though three days may feel short, with careful planning, it's possible to get a true sense of the country, making this trip feel both rich and fulfilling. And the best part? You won't feel like you've missed anything important. It's all about pacing and enjoying each moment without the pressure of rushing through the sights. Whether you're wandering Prague's streets, marveling at the views in Český Krumlov, or breathing in the fresh air of Bohemian Switzerland, you'll leave with memories that last a lifetime.

Extensive Weeklong Journeys: A Detailed 7-Day Guide

If you've got an entire week to explore the Czech Republic, you're in for a treat. A week offers the perfect balance between delving deep into Prague's history and culture, while also venturing out to some of the country's most stunning towns, castles, and natural wonders. When I spent a week there, I was struck by how the country offers such a rich variety of experiences, and even after seven days, I knew I could easily have stayed longer. Here's how I would recommend spending a week in the Czech Republic for a journey that blends city excitement, historical exploration, and outdoor beauty.

Start your first two days in Prague, the country's bustling capital. Begin with the iconic sights like Prague Castle, St. Vitus Cathedral, and Charles Bridge. The castle, perched high above the city, is a must-see and will give you a deep dive into the history of the Czech monarchy. I recommend spending a good part of your first day exploring the Old Town, particularly the Astronomical Clock and the Old Town Square. It's here you'll get a feel for the city's medieval charm, and it's also a great spot for lunch or a coffee at one of the charming cafes. In the afternoon, head over to the Jewish Quarter, where you can visit the synagogues and the poignant Jewish Museum. To wind down, head across the river to Petrín Hill, which offers not only a peaceful escape but also spectacular views of the city. The second day in Prague could be devoted to more relaxed experiences, such as exploring the art scene at the National Gallery or enjoying the city's famous beer culture in one of the traditional beer halls.

On day three, it's time to leave the city behind and head toward Český Krumlov. This picturesque town, often compared to Prague for its beauty, is like something out of a storybook. The town is a UNESCO World Heritage Site and is best known for its stunning medieval architecture and the mighty Český Krumlov Castle. I recommend a leisurely day wandering the cobblestone streets, taking in the lovely mix of Renaissance, Gothic, and Baroque styles. The castle here is not only a historic gem, but it also offers spectacular views of the Vltava River that winds through the town. You can also take a relaxing boat trip along the river or hike up to the castle gardens for a peaceful afternoon. Český Krumlov has an undeniable charm, and I guarantee you'll find it hard to leave after just one day.

Day four should be dedicated to the Bohemian and Moravian regions, each filled with distinct landscapes and sights. I suggest a visit to the town of Telč, a stunning town square surrounded by colorful Renaissance-style houses, which is just a few hours from Český Krumlov. The main square is a delight, and the beautiful Telč Castle, with its picturesque gardens, is another highlight. From Telč, head north to the town of Kutná Hora. This is where you'll find the famous Sedlec Ossuary, a chapel decorated with thousands of human bones, creating a macabre but fascinating atmosphere. It's a somber and surreal experience, but one I found to be uniquely memorable. You can also spend time walking around Kutná Hora's historic center, with its impressive St. Barbara's Cathedral.

On day five, make your way to the Czech countryside, where you'll discover the natural beauty of the Czech Republic. Visit the Krkonošsko (Giant Mountains) National Park, located in the northeastern part of the country. This area is ideal for anyone who loves hiking and outdoor adventures. I personally spent a day hiking up the Sněžka Mountain, the highest peak in the Czech Republic, and the views from the top were nothing short of breathtaking. The park has well-maintained trails, with various difficulty levels, so it's perfect for all kinds of adventurers. After a day of exploring nature, unwind at one of the local spas or enjoy a hearty Czech meal in a traditional mountain hut. For day six, head to the

Moravian region, which is famed for its vineyards and stunning castles. I spent the day in Mikulov, a charming town surrounded by vineyards. The Mikulov Castle here is perched on a hill and offers panoramic views of the surrounding vineyards. If you're a wine lover, this is the perfect spot to take a wine tour and sample some of the country's finest wines. I found the mix of wine tasting and history to be a relaxing yet engaging way to explore the region. The towns around Mikulov are also lovely for wandering, with quiet streets and picturesque squares that are perfect for soaking in the slow pace of life.

On your final day, take it easy in the town of Brno, the second-largest city in the Czech Republic, and an often-overlooked gem. Brno is much less touristy than Prague but has plenty to offer in terms of culture and history. One of the most interesting things I did was visit the Villa Tugendhat, a modernist architectural marvel that is a UNESCO World Heritage Site. The city also has a fascinating underground labyrinth, and the Špilberk Castle offers great views of the city. Brno also has a great food scene, with a growing number of hip cafes and restaurants where you can sample Czech dishes with a modern twist. The relaxed vibe of Brno was the perfect way to end my week in the Czech Republic before heading back to Prague for my flight.

By the time your week in the Czech Republic is up, you'll have experienced a perfect blend of history, culture, nature, and small-town charm. It's a trip that offers something for everyone—whether you're a history buff, nature lover, or just someone who wants to slow down and take in the beauty of the Czech countryside. The country's diverse offerings are bound to leave you with memories you'll cherish long after you've returned home.

2-Week Comprehensive Tour of the Czech Republic

If you have two weeks to explore the Czech Republic, you're in for a truly enriching experience that will take you from vibrant cities steeped in history to the quiet charm of the countryside, with plenty of natural beauty and cultural highlights in between. The country offers such a wealth of diverse attractions that two weeks is just the right amount of time to get a comprehensive, fulfilling glimpse into what it has to offer. Whether you're wandering through the cobbled streets of medieval towns, hiking in lush national parks, or enjoying the warmth of a local pub, there's so much to absorb. Here's how I'd recommend spending your two weeks in this fascinating country.

The first few days are perfect for exploring Prague, a city that never gets old no matter how many times you visit. On the first day, start with the essentials: Prague Castle, the Charles Bridge, and the Old Town Square. I was completely captivated by the city's mix of Gothic and Baroque architecture, particularly around the Old Town. Make sure you spend time exploring the Old Town's hidden corners—sometimes the best views come when you're not looking for them. The second day could be spent soaking in Prague's art and culture—visit the National Gallery or the Museum of Communism, which provides a unique perspective on the country's 20th-century history.

You'll also want to take a break in one of the many cozy cafes, sipping on some Czech coffee or indulging in a slice of traditional koláče. By your third day, delve deeper into Prague's quirky side—check out the John Lennon Wall or take a walk along the Vltava River. And don't forget to sample some Czech beer at a local brewery; Prague is world-renowned for its beer culture. I recommend a visit to U Fleku, one of the oldest breweries in the city. By day four, it's time to head outside the capital and experience some of the Czech countryside. Start with a day trip to Český Krumlov, one of the country's most picturesque towns. The castle here is sprawling, and its gardens offer magnificent views over the Vltava River. The town's medieval charm will have you feeling like you've stepped back in time.

Don't rush through—it's the perfect place to slow down, wander, and even take a boat ride down the river. On day five, travel a little further to the charming town of Telč, known for its beautiful Renaissance town square. The pastel-colored houses along the square are like something from a painting, and the Telč Castle adds an extra layer of beauty to the scene. From Telč, head toward Kutná Hora, a town renowned for its historical significance and its eerie, yet fascinating, Sedlec Ossuary—also known as the Bone Church—decorated with thousands of human bones. Spend the night in Kutná Hora, and explore its other historical landmarks like St.

Barbara's Cathedral. After soaking in the southern and central regions, take a detour into the Czech countryside for the next few days. On day seven, head to the Krkonoš Mountains, a paradise for outdoor enthusiasts. I spent an unforgettable day hiking in the Krkonošsko National Park, where the landscape shifts from dense forests to alpine meadows. The highlight of the day was hiking to Sněžka, the highest peak in the Czech Republic, where I was treated to panoramic views that stretched for miles. After all that hiking, treat yourself to some well-earned relaxation in one of the cozy mountain huts or enjoy a spa experience in one of the nearby resorts.

Now that you've seen the natural beauty of the Czech Republic, your next few days could be spent exploring the rich cultural history of Moravia. Day eight takes you to the city of Brno, the Czech Republic's second-largest city. I really enjoyed the vibe here—it's quieter than Prague, but it offers a fascinating mix of modern and historic architecture. Make sure to visit the famous Villa Tugendhat, a UNESCO World Heritage Site, and explore the underground labyrinth of cellars beneath the city. After Brno, you'll want to head to Mikulov, a small town famous for its vineyards. The Mikulov Castle offers stunning views over the surrounding countryside, and the wine tours here are among the best in the country. Spend the next few days enjoying the slow pace of life in these wine regions, tasting local wines, and exploring the picturesque town of Znojmo, with its lovely medieval streets and nearby natural reserves.

For days eleven and twelve, head towards the region of Moravian Slovakia, which is home to an array of charming towns like Kyjov and the UNESCO-listed Lednice-Valtice Cultural Landscape. The Lednice Castle, surrounded by sprawling gardens and parks, is one of the most stunning castles I've ever visited. I recommend taking a boat ride along the canal that cuts through the grounds, or you can rent a bike and cycle around the landscape. It's an area that feels peaceful and untouched, and you'll find plenty of time to reflect on the trip so far. On day thirteen, head back toward the Bohemian region, making a stop at Hradec Králové. This city offers a mix of Renaissance, Baroque, and modernist architecture, and is a great place to relax before heading back to Prague.

You'll find plenty of parks, cafes, and places to stroll without the bustle of the major tourist centers. From there, head back to Prague for your final day in the country. Spend this last day soaking in the atmosphere at places you may have missed earlier in your trip, such as the Vyšehrad fortress, which offers stunning views of the city, or perhaps take a boat cruise along the Vltava River. It's the perfect way to reflect on your journey through the Czech Republic.

CHAPTER 15

Essential Information

When you're traveling to a new country, especially one as rich in history and culture as the Czech Republic, having the right information at your fingertips can make all the difference. Over the years, I've learned that a little planning ahead can save you a lot of time, money, and frustration. This chapter is designed to be your go-to resource for the essential practical details that will help you navigate the Czech Republic with ease. From staying connected and finding free attractions to understanding the ins and outs of transportation and what to expect when you shop or dine out, we'll cover all the basics you need to ensure your trip runs smoothly.

If you've ever traveled to a new place, you know how important it is to stay connected. Whether you need to find your way around with maps or keep in touch with family and friends back home, having reliable internet and communication options can be a real game-changer. I'll share everything I've learned about staying connected in the Czech Republic, including tips on local SIM cards, Wi-Fi availability, and how to use various apps to make your experience more seamless. But it's not just about internet and tech—it's also about experiencing the best of what the country offers without breaking the bank. That's why I'll walk you through some of the best free attractions the country has to offer, from stunning parks to historical sites, as well as the paid attractions that are worth every penny. Knowing when places are open, how to rent a car, or whether you want to take a guided tour versus exploring on your own can change the way you experience a destination.

Plus, I'll guide you through some of the most useful apps and websites that I've found to be indispensable while traveling here—tools that can save you from confusion and help you make the most of your time in the Czech Republic. Finally, we'll finish up with some important information to remember when preparing to leave, including customs regulations and a departure checklist that ensures you're not missing anything as you wrap up your trip.

By the time you finish this chapter, you'll feel prepared for everything the Czech Republic has to offer—practical details, local insights, and everything in between. Let's dive into the essential information that will make your travel experience a whole lot easier and more enjoyable.

Internet, Communication, and Staying Connected

When I first visited the Czech Republic, one of the first things I noticed was how easy it was to stay connected. In today's world, having reliable access to the internet and knowing your communication options is crucial, whether you're navigating a city, staying in touch with loved ones, or simply looking up information on the fly. The Czech Republic, like much of Europe, has a well-established infrastructure that makes staying connected surprisingly smooth. But just like in any foreign country, knowing how to get online and how to use communication tools efficiently can save you from a lot of stress.

First off, you'll find that the Czech Republic has excellent Wi-Fi coverage, especially in major cities like Prague, Brno, and Plzeň. Most hotels, cafes, restaurants, and even some public transport systems offer free Wi-Fi, which makes it easy to check your email or catch up on social media during a coffee break. I remember the first time I sat down at a café in Prague's Old Town, and the Wi-Fi password was written on a chalkboard on the wall. That's the level of accessibility you can expect here. Public areas like parks, squares, and even some metro stations also offer free Wi-Fi. However, keep in mind that public Wi-Fi can sometimes be a bit spotty or slow, so it's always a good idea to check the connection before relying on it for anything important.

If you're planning to stay longer or need more consistent connectivity, purchasing a local SIM card is one of the best options. I've done this every time I've visited, and it's been a game changer. Local providers like T-Mobile Czech Republic, Vodafone Czech Republic, and O2 offer a variety of prepaid plans that are straightforward to set up and quite affordable. I picked up a SIM card at the airport upon arrival, which was quick and easy, and I was good to go in just a few minutes. The data plans are usually generous and often include unlimited texts and calls within the Czech Republic, as well as affordable roaming options across Europe. Most of the major phone stores or even kiosks in shopping malls will sell these cards, and you'll find that customer service is usually helpful in English.

Free Tourist Attractions and Paid Tourist Attractions

One of the things I love most about traveling in the Czech Republic is that there's no shortage of amazing things to do, whether you're on a budget or looking to splurge a little. The balance of free and paid attractions here makes it easy to create an itinerary that fits both your interests and your wallet. I remember, on my first trip, I was both amazed by how many things I could do for free, and at the same time, I discovered some incredible experiences that were definitely worth the price of admission.

Let me start with the free attractions, which, for me, were a pleasant surprise. If you're like me and enjoy just walking around to get a feel for a city, you'll be pleased to know that the Czech Republic offers plenty of things to see without paying a cent. In Prague, for instance, walking around the Old Town (Staré Město) is a must. You don't need a ticket to admire the stunning architecture or explore the winding streets lined with historical buildings. The Astronomical Clock in Prague's Old Town Square is another great example; you can enjoy watching the clock perform its mechanical show every hour, without spending anything. If you're into history, wandering through Charles Bridge (Karlův most) is another must-do experience. Spanning the Vltava River, it's free to walk across, and the views of Prague Castle, the river, and the city's skyline are breathtaking.

The same goes for Prague Castle itself. While it does charge for access to the buildings and museums inside the castle grounds, the castle complex and its grounds are free to roam. The gardens and courtyards are open to the public, and you can get a sense of the castle's grandeur just by walking around the perimeter. I spent a few hours soaking in the history and the peacefulness of the area without spending anything. In addition, there are several free museums that are worth checking out, like the National Museum of Czech Music, where the admission is free on the first Monday of every month. Another free gem I discovered was Petrin Hill, located just southwest of Prague Castle. After a fun climb up, you're rewarded with panoramic views of the city. The park itself is beautiful, with plenty of green space for picnics or just enjoying the outdoors. While there is a fee to visit the Petrin Tower (often referred to as Prague's "mini Eiffel Tower"), simply walking around the hill and enjoying the gardens is completely free.

Now, when it comes to paid attractions, I found that many are well worth the price, offering a unique glimpse into the country's history, art, and culture. One of the first places I visited was the Prague Castle's St. Vitus Cathedral. The entrance is free to the cathedral itself, but if you want to explore the interior and see the tombs of kings and emperors, you'll need to buy a ticket. The fee is modest, and it's worth it for the chance to explore one of Europe's most beautiful Gothic cathedrals.

Another paid experience that I highly recommend is the Old Jewish Cemetery in Prague, one of the oldest surviving Jewish cemeteries in Europe. It's a peaceful and thought-provoking place, filled with centuries of history. While visiting the cemetery is free, the small museum located on the grounds has a reasonable entrance fee and provides insightful context about the Jewish community in Prague. The nearby Jewish Museum is also a great stop, offering a deep dive into Jewish history and culture in the region. If you're looking for something a bit more modern, I suggest heading to the National Gallery in Prague. There's an admission fee, but the exhibitions are impressive, showcasing Czech and international art from the medieval period to the present day. The gallery is housed in several locations, so depending on your interests, you can spend a whole day or just a few hours exploring the rich collection. It's located in the Veletržní Palác, which is a short walk from the Holesovice train station, or a quick tram ride from central Prague. For something a little more unique, I recommend visiting the Prague Beer Museum. It's a small but fascinating stop where you can learn about the Czech Republic's deep love for beer and taste different varieties from local breweries. The entrance fee here is small, and it's a fun way to experience an integral part of Czech culture.

Outside of Prague, there are plenty of paid attractions to explore as well. In Český Krumlov, a charming medieval town south of Prague, the castle is one of the main highlights. While wandering the town and admiring the views of the Vltava River are free, you'll need to purchase tickets to enter the castle and its stunning gardens. The guided tours are informative, and the castle's interior is a peek into the aristocratic history of the region. Similarly, in Brno, the Špilberk Castle offers both paid and free options. While you can stroll around the castle's exterior and enjoy the views, the museum inside requires a ticket. It's worth it, though, for the chance to explore the history of the castle, which once served as a fortress and later a prison.

Opening Hours for Major Attractions

When I first set foot in the Czech Republic, one of the most pleasant surprises was how accessible many of the country's most iconic attractions were—both in terms of cost and their opening hours. I quickly learned that there are a number of major sights that don't charge an entrance fee, and they have generous opening times that make it easy to explore at your own pace. The Czech Republic has made it possible for travelers to enjoy a rich cultural experience without feeling rushed, all while accommodating different schedules. In Prague, the Old Town (Staré Město) is one of those iconic places that you can visit at any time of day, and it won't cost you a thing.

The Old Town Square, with its impressive historical architecture, is always open to the public. There's no entry fee, so you can wander the cobblestone streets and admire the beauty of buildings like the Town Hall and the Church of Our Lady before Týn, all at your leisure. The square comes to life in the early morning with fewer crowds, making it a great time to enjoy the peaceful vibe before the tourist rush begins. The famous Astronomical Clock is located here, and although there's a fee for the tower, watching the clock's mechanical show every hour is completely free. For another amazing, free experience, head to Charles Bridge (Karlův most), which connects Prague's Old Town to Malá Strana (Lesser Town). Open 24 hours a day, this iconic bridge is always accessible for a stroll. Whether you're walking across to catch a view of Prague Castle or simply soaking in the riverside atmosphere, you'll find that it offers a picturesque, free experience any time of day. I loved walking across the bridge at sunrise when the city was still quiet, and the early light made everything look even more magical.

Another fantastic free experience is visiting the vast grounds of Prague Castle. Though it costs money to enter some parts of the castle, like St. Vitus Cathedral or the Old Royal Palace, you can still roam around the castle's gardens, courtyards, and perimeter without paying a cent. I spent an afternoon wandering around the castle complex and taking in the views of the city below. The castle grounds are open every day, typically from 6:00 AM to 10:00 PM, giving you plenty of time to visit, whether you prefer an early morning visit or an evening walk.

If you're looking for a little greenery to balance out your city exploration, Petrin Hill is another wonderful spot that's always open. Located just southwest of the castle, it's an easy walk from there or a short ride by tram (take tram #22 or #23). While there's a fee to ascend the Petrin Tower, which offers stunning panoramic views of Prague, the hill itself is free to visit. I took a leisurely stroll through the gardens and paths, which offered a peaceful break from the hustle of the city center. The hill is especially popular for locals and tourists alike for a relaxing afternoon outdoors.

Car Rental recommendations

When I first considered renting a car in the Czech Republic, I had some reservations. Would driving be as easy as it seemed? Would navigating unfamiliar roads be overwhelming? But after spending a bit of time exploring, I found that renting a car is actually one of the best ways to fully experience the country. The Czech Republic offers an excellent network of highways and roads, making it ideal for those who want to venture beyond the cities and explore quaint towns, picturesque villages, and stunning countryside. From the rolling hills of Moravia to the fairytale-like streets of Český Krumlov, having a car gave me the freedom to visit these less accessible but equally remarkable destinations at my own pace.

First, let me walk you through the basics of car rentals in the Czech Republic. Renting a car here is straightforward, and there are numerous well-known international rental companies, as well as local ones, offering a range of vehicles. For most tourists, the rental process is very similar to what you'd experience in other European countries, but there are a few important things to keep in mind. When renting a car, I found that the most common requirements are being at least 21 years old (with a few companies requiring you to be 23 or older for certain cars), having a valid driver's license, and a credit card for the deposit. If you're from the U.S. or another non-EU country, you'll need an International Driving Permit (IDP) in addition to your home country's driver's license. That said, driving in the Czech Republic is fairly easy, with well-marked roads, clear signage, and drivers who are generally polite and follow traffic rules.

As for the cost, the range for car rentals can vary greatly depending on the season, the car model, and the rental company. On average, you can expect to pay anywhere between $30 to $70 per day for a small economy car (like a Volkswagen

Polo or a Škoda Fabia). This is the ideal option if you're looking for something practical and easy to navigate through city streets. For larger cars or SUVs, expect to pay anywhere from $60 to $120 per day. Keep in mind that prices can spike during peak tourist seasons, especially in the summer and around holidays.

One rental agency I used and can highly recommend is Sixt Rent a Car, which has a solid reputation in the Czech Republic. They have multiple locations, including at Prague Václav Havel Airport and in the city center. I picked up my car from their office in downtown Prague, located at Sixt Prague - Central Station, at Wilsonova 300/8, 120 00 Praha 2. The staff was very helpful and spoke English fluently, which made the process easy and quick. Their vehicles are well-maintained, and they offer everything from small city cars to luxury models and even vans for larger groups. The price for a standard compact car was around $40 per day, and they offer useful add-ons like GPS, additional insurance, and child car seats. You can reach Sixt by phone at +420 257 053 360, or visit their website at www.sixt.com to check availability and book in advance. If you're arriving by public transport, the Central Station location is just a few minutes' walk from Prague's main train station, which is well connected by metro (Line C, Hlavní nádraží station) and trams. If you're flying into Prague, Sixt also has a desk at the airport, which is a convenient option if you want to pick up your car as soon as you arrive. The prices at the airport are typically a bit higher, but the convenience of getting straight to your car after a long flight is hard to beat.

Another great option for car rentals in the Czech Republic is Europcar, which also has a presence in major cities like Prague, Brno, and Ostrava, as well as at the airport. Europcar is well known for its wide variety of cars and excellent customer service. I rented from their Prague Airport location, where I found their staff to be both professional and knowledgeable. The price for a compact car here was about $45 per day, and they also offered a range of options, including electric cars, which is a nice choice for eco-conscious travelers. You can contact Europcar at +420 220 510 302, or book online at www.europcar.com.

For a more local experience, I also rented from Czechocar, a local rental company with a reputation for providing friendly service and affordable rates. They have an office in Prague, located at Žitná 602/3, 110 00 Praha 1, just a short walk from Wenceslas Square. The price here was around $30 per day for a small car, and they offer useful amenities like unlimited mileage, which is great if you plan to explore the country thoroughly. The staff at Czechocar is particularly helpful if you have questions about navigating Czech roads or recommendations for places to visit. You can reach them at +420 222 246 933, or check out their website at www.czechocar.com for bookings.

Once you've got your car, getting around the Czech Republic is easy. In Prague, driving can be a bit tricky in the city center due to narrow streets and heavy traffic, but once you're outside the capital, the road system is straightforward and efficient. I particularly enjoyed driving in the Czech countryside, where the roads are well-maintained, and the scenery is simply stunning. When you're driving on highways or rural roads, keep an eye out for road signs indicating speed limits (which are clearly marked) and always have a highway vignette (toll sticker) if you plan to use highways. These can be purchased at gas stations or online.

For those planning longer road trips, I recommend using a GPS or navigation app like Google Maps, as some of the smaller towns may not have clear road signs in English. If you don't want to rely on your phone's data, most car rental agencies offer GPS units for an additional fee, which I found handy for navigating unfamiliar areas.

If you're planning to explore the charming towns like Český Krumlov or Kutná Hora, renting a car is by far the easiest and most convenient way to travel. Public transportation is great for getting to major cities, but when you want to visit less-visited destinations, a rental car gives you the flexibility to go wherever you want. Plus, the open road is one of the best ways to experience the true beauty of the Czech Republic!

Guided Tours vs. Self-Guided Explorations

When I visited the Czech Republic, one of the most exciting things to consider was how to explore this beautiful country. Should I take a guided tour and let an expert walk me through the historical wonders of Prague, or venture off on my own for a more independent and flexible experience? After spending time in both types of explorations, I've found that each approach has its own appeal, and it really depends on what kind of experience you're seeking.

Guided tours in the Czech Republic can be an incredible way to absorb the rich history, culture, and hidden gems of the country. The knowledge and passion of the local guides give you a deeper connection to the places you're visiting, which can be hard to replicate on your own. For instance, when I took a walking tour through the Old Town of Prague, the guide shared fascinating details about the history of the area, including the stories behind famous landmarks like the Astronomical Clock and Old Town Square. I never would have known about the hidden medieval alleyways and their significance without the guide's input. It was like hearing the secrets of the city that only the locals know.

For guided tours, there are a number of reliable and well-organized options to consider. One highly recommended company is Prague Walks (praguewalks.com). Their Old Town walking tour, which lasts about 2 hours, costs around $25 USD per person. It takes you through Prague's most iconic spots, and I especially appreciated that the group size was small enough to make the experience feel personal. If you're looking for something more in-depth, you can join their Castle District tour for around $35 USD, which explores the Prague Castle and its impressive grounds. They also offer private tours, which can be customized based on your interests, whether you want to focus on art, history, or local culture.

The tours are available in multiple languages, and their guides are not only knowledgeable but passionate about sharing the Czech Republic's past. Prague Walks departs from their office near the Old Town, which is very centrally located and easy to get to via public transport or even walking from most central accommodations.

If you're looking for a unique and slightly more adventurous experience, I'd recommend trying out the Beer and Brewery Tour with Viator (viator.com). The Czech Republic is famous for its beer, and this guided tour will take you to local breweries to sample different types and learn about the brewing process. Prices for this tour range from $50 to $70 USD, depending on the length of the tour and whether it's a small group or private. This tour is a fun way to immerse yourself in Czech culture, and you'll also get to try some delicious local dishes that pair perfectly with the brews. It's a great way to see a side of

Prague you might otherwise miss, especially if you're a fan of beer.

On the other hand, self-guided exploration is another fantastic way to see the Czech Republic, and in many ways, it suits the independent traveler like myself. Having the freedom to go wherever you want, whenever you want, can be incredibly liberating. For instance, I loved spending an afternoon wandering through the quiet streets of the Vinohrady district in Prague, admiring its stunning architecture without the pressure of sticking to a schedule. Self-guided tours also allow you to linger in places you find particularly interesting, whether it's a hidden café or a small museum. Plus, it's often much cheaper than booking a guided tour.

Self-guided exploration in the Czech Republic is made even easier with a range of useful apps and websites. The Czech Tourism website (czechtourism.com) is an excellent resource, offering detailed information about landmarks, activities, and events across the country. You can easily use it to plan your own itinerary, and I found it particularly helpful for locating lesser-known spots that don't always appear in guidebooks. For more specific city information, I relied heavily on the Prague City App (praguecityapp.com), which includes interactive maps, tourist attractions, public transport timetables, and even restaurant suggestions. The app works offline, which is incredibly useful when you're exploring without a data connection.

There are also audioguide apps, such as izi.TRAVEL, which provides self-guided tours for numerous attractions in Prague and beyond. You can download specific tours directly to your phone and listen to them at your own pace. For example, I downloaded a tour of the Prague Castle, and it gave me detailed descriptions of each area of the castle complex. It was like having a personal guide right in my pocket.

Now, while I enjoyed the flexibility of self-guided exploration, there are a few things to keep in mind. Some attractions, such as the Prague Castle or the Jewish Quarter, can get a bit overwhelming to navigate without the historical context that a guide provides. I realized that when I visited the Old Jewish Cemetery on my own, I didn't fully appreciate the depth of its significance until I went back with a guide the following day. A guide can really bring those sites to life and offer insights that I might have missed on my own.

The best part of self-guided exploration, however, is the freedom to choose exactly what interests you. You can create your own itinerary, whether you want to visit museums, try different local dishes, or just stroll through a peaceful park. On days when I wasn't feeling up to a formal tour, I'd simply grab a map and set off to discover Prague on foot, and I was constantly surprised by how many beautiful and interesting spots I stumbled upon.

In the end, whether you go for a guided tour or a self-guided adventure really depends on your style of travel. If you're someone who enjoys structure and learning from experts, guided tours are a fantastic choice. But if you prefer more flexibility and the thrill of discovering things on your own, self-guided exploration can be just as rewarding. Both options provide unique ways to experience the Czech Republic, and I'm sure whichever you choose, you'll find plenty to see and do.

Useful Apps and Websites

During my time in the Czech Republic, I quickly realized how much easier it is to get around and experience everything the country has to offer when you make use of a few well-chosen apps and websites. Whether you're navigating the transport system, booking accommodation, or trying to find the best local restaurants, having the right tools on hand can make a world of difference.

One app that became indispensable during my travels is Public Transport Prague (PID Lítačka). This app is a must if you plan to use public transportation in Prague. It provides up-to-date timetables, route planning, and real-time information on buses, trams, and metro services. I found it especially helpful when I needed to check for delays or find the quickest route to my destination. What's even better is that you can purchase tickets directly from the app, which saved me from standing in long lines at ticket machines. You can choose from different ticket types, depending on the length of your stay and travel needs, and there's also an option for buying tickets valid for multiple days. The app is available in English, which made everything much more accessible for me.

Another app that became quite handy is Uber. While public transport is great in the cities, there were times when I needed a quicker or more direct route to my destination. Uber is available in Prague, and it's very reliable. The app allows you to select the type of car you need, whether it's a regular ride or a larger vehicle, which was perfect for when I had extra luggage. It was also useful for getting from Prague to nearby towns or attractions when public transportation wasn't as convenient. The prices are reasonable, and the app lets you pay directly from your phone, so it's seamless and hassle-free. For finding great places to eat, Zomato (formerly known as UrbanSpoon) is a top app. It helps you search for restaurants, read reviews, and check out menus. I loved being able to browse local recommendations from other travelers and get a feel for the ambiance and quality of food before even stepping inside. What's great about Zomato is that it has a wide selection of restaurants, ranging from fine dining to local eateries, and the ratings are generally quite accurate. You can even book tables directly through the app, which is incredibly convenient, especially when you're visiting a popular spot.

When it comes to booking accommodation, I found Booking.com and Airbnb to be indispensable. Booking.com offers a wide range of hotels, guesthouses, and apartments throughout the country, and the reviews are quite reliable. The app allows you to filter by accessibility features, room types, and amenities, which made it easier to find the perfect place to stay. I used it frequently for last-minute bookings, and the process was smooth and straightforward. If you prefer a more homely experience, Airbnb offers a great selection of apartments, houses, and unique stays, especially in more remote areas outside Prague. Both platforms have English-language options and offer cancellation flexibility, which can be a lifesaver when travel plans change unexpectedly.

For finding cultural events, exhibitions, and activities, GoOut is a great app. I used it to check out concerts, theater performances, and local festivals happening during my stay. It gives you access to a calendar of events across the Czech Republic, allowing you to plan your days around things that interest you. You can also buy tickets through the app, making it very convenient if you're looking to experience Czech culture beyond the usual tourist sites. A site I used frequently to plan my visits to museums and historical sites was Czech Tourism. Their website is incredibly detailed and offers information about events, recommended itineraries, and tips for travelers. The website is available in English, which was helpful for me, as it's packed with useful details on where to go, what to see, and how to get there. I used it to learn about hidden gems and to plan day trips outside of Prague, and it always had the latest updates on opening hours, closures, and special events. For anyone looking for information on accessible travel, I'd recommend checking out Access Travel Czech Republic. This website is a fantastic resource for travelers with disabilities. It provides detailed information about wheelchair-accessible routes, public transport, and accommodations. I found it helpful for navigating the country's accessibility features and ensuring I had all the necessary information to make my trip as comfortable as possible.

Lastly, for currency exchange and keeping track of money, XE Currency is a handy app. The Czech Republic uses the Czech koruna, not the euro, so I found it useful to keep track of exchange rates and calculate how much things would cost in my home currency. XE Currency allows you to store exchange rates offline, which was great for those times I didn't have internet access but needed to know whether I was getting a good deal on a souvenir.

Having these apps and websites at my disposal helped me feel more confident while exploring the Czech Republic. They made getting around, booking accommodations, and finding things to do so much easier. If you're planning to visit, I definitely recommend downloading a few of these to make your trip smoother and more enjoyable. With everything from public transport to local events at your fingertips, you'll be able to spend less time planning and more time exploring this beautiful country.

Departure Checklist and Customs Regulations

As my time in the Czech Republic came to a close, I realized that preparing for departure requires just as much attention to detail as the journey itself. The process of leaving any country can feel a bit overwhelming, especially when it comes to customs regulations and the checklist of things to take care of before heading to the airport. But as I learned during my trip, a little bit of preparation makes all the difference and ensures that your exit from the Czech Republic is as smooth as your arrival. First things first, it's essential to double-check your passport and travel documents. If you're leaving the country by plane, you'll need your passport, and depending on your nationality, you may need a visa.

Even though the Czech Republic is part of the Schengen Area, and border checks between countries in the area are typically minimal, always be sure to carry the documents you used when entering the country. Also, make sure that your passport is valid for at least three months beyond your intended departure date. I remember the anxiety I felt when I realized I hadn't checked the validity of my passport before traveling, so this is something that's easy to overlook but incredibly important.

One thing that caught me off guard was the baggage limits and regulations. When traveling internationally, it's crucial to know what you can and cannot bring with you. The Czech Republic, like many European countries, adheres to the standard international flight restrictions regarding liquids, sharp objects, and other prohibited items. But there are also specific rules for bringing in goods or souvenirs, particularly when it comes to alcohol, tobacco, or products made from protected animals. If you bought any goods while in the Czech Republic, particularly traditional items like crystal, make sure you know whether they are subject to export restrictions. I found out the hard way that certain antiques or art pieces can be restricted, so always check before you buy something you plan to take home. Customs regulations are another area to pay close attention to. As a non-EU traveler, I had to make sure I understood the duty-free allowance and what I could bring back into my home country. The Czech Republic, as part of the EU, has specific guidelines for what's allowed to be brought into other EU countries and non-EU countries.

For example, alcohol and tobacco are often subject to limits, and if you're carrying large sums of money, you might have to declare it. If you're traveling with any goods that could be considered "commercial quantities," like multiple bottles of liquor, make sure you have receipts for everything. It can save you from potential fines or complications at customs, and I found this particularly helpful when I was bringing back some local wine from Moravia. As my departure day grew nearer, I started to think about the practical aspects of leaving, such as transportation to the airport. Prague's Václav Havel Airport is well connected by public transport, so getting there from the city center is straightforward. I opted for the Airport Express bus, which departs from the main train station and takes you directly to the airport in about 30 minutes. Alternatively, taxis and ridesharing services like Uber are widely available, though they tend to be a bit pricier.

I personally preferred the bus because it was easy, reliable, and inexpensive, but it's worth considering all your options, depending on where you're staying and your departure time. One of the things that I found most helpful in preparing for departure was organizing my belongings the night before. That way, when it was time to leave, I could simply double-check my documents and be ready to go. The day of your departure can get hectic, so I recommend laying out your travel essentials, making sure all your belongings are packed, and taking a last walk through your accommodation to ensure you didn't forget anything important. This is also a great time to check the weather forecast and dress accordingly for your flight, especially if you're traveling to a different climate. Before you leave the Czech Republic, it's also a good idea to handle any remaining payments or bills. Some accommodations might charge you for extras, like late check-out fees or minibar items, so check your bill and take care of any outstanding balances before you head to the airport. I found that paying in Czech korunas, the local currency, is often the most straightforward way to avoid extra fees, especially if you're staying at a hotel that doesn't accept credit cards or prefers cash.

CONCLUSION

As I reflect on my time traveling through the Czech Republic, I can confidently say that it's a destination that offers something for everyone. Whether you're a history buff, a lover of architecture, or simply someone looking to enjoy beautiful scenery, the country provides experiences that are as varied as they are rich. The cobblestone streets of Prague, the stunning castles scattered throughout the countryside, and the picturesque towns like Český Krumlov all offer a chance to step back in time while also embracing the vibrant culture that's so alive today.

For anyone planning to visit, the Czech Republic is not only affordable but also incredibly accessible. The public transportation system, whether by tram, metro, or bus, is reliable and easy to use, making it simple to navigate both within cities and to the surrounding areas. If you're someone who enjoys history, you'll find endless stories waiting to be uncovered, from the ancient Prague Castle to the poignant Jewish Quarter. Nature lovers will appreciate the country's stunning landscapes, whether it's the serene countryside or the dramatic cliffs near the town of Adršpach-Teplice Rocks.

But beyond just the sites and the beautiful scenery, what makes the Czech Republic truly special is its atmosphere. There's a certain calmness to the country, a relaxed pace of life that invites you to slow down and take in the details around you. It's a place where you can wander aimlessly down a narrow alley in Prague and suddenly stumble upon a charming café or a hidden courtyard filled with flowers. It's a country that, despite its rich history and bustling cities, still feels incredibly approachable.

In my experience, whether you're opting for a guided tour to gain deeper insights into the places you visit or you're exploring on your own, the Czech Republic caters to every kind of traveler.

Guided tours are a great way to tap into local knowledge and get a deeper understanding of the country's history and culture. However, if you prefer more independence, self-guided tours with the help of apps or guidebooks are just as rewarding. Both options have their perks, and either way, you're sure to uncover something unforgettable.

Ultimately, the Czech Republic is a country that invites exploration, whether you're strolling through the streets of Prague or venturing off the beaten path. It's a place where you can immerse yourself in centuries of history, indulge in delicious food and drink, and connect with locals who are welcoming and proud of their heritage. Every corner of this country tells a story, and I can guarantee that if you make the effort to explore, you'll leave with a deeper appreciation for its unique charm.

As I look back, I feel a sense of gratitude for all the moments of discovery and awe that this country provided, and I'm sure anyone who visits will find something special that resonates with them. The Czech Republic may be small in size, but it's vast in experiences—something you'll realize as soon as you start to explore.

Printed in Great Britain
by Amazon